WE WERE PERFECT PARENTS *until* WE HAD CHILDREN

60 000 VILLAGE FAMILIES SHARE THEIR WISDOM

Vanessa Raphaely & Karin Schimke

Jonathan Ball Publishers
JOHANNESBURG & CAPE TOWN

All rights reserved.
No part of this publication may be reproduced or transmitted, in any form or by any means, without the prior written permission of the publisher or copyright holder.

Text © Vanessa Raphaely & Karin Schimke (2024)
Cover illustration Minky Stapleton
Internal illustrations Minky Stapleton
Published edition © Jonathan Ball Publishers (2024)

Published in South Africa in 2024 by
JONATHAN BALL PUBLISHERS
A division of Media24 (Pty) Ltd
PO Box 33977
Jeppestown
2043

ISBN 978-1-77619-262-5

ebook ISBN 978-1-77619-263-2

Every effort has been made to trace the copyright holders and to obtain their permission for the use of copyright material. The publishers apologise for any errors or omissions and would be grateful to be notified of any corrections that should be incorporated in future editions of this book.

jonathanball.co.za
x.com/JonathanBallPub
facebook.com/JonathanBallPublishers

Cover by Minky Stapelton
Design and typesetting by Melanie Kriel
Set in Demos Next

Dedicated to
Every single Villager and the Admins,
Creative Team and Boost Crews,
with so much love and thanks.

Contents

Introduction: It takes a Village — vii
Some pointers about this book — xi

Talking about talking — **1**
1 It starts with you (and us!) — 3
2 Help! Who is this alien? — 19
3 Compassionate boys, feisty girls — 37
4 Shouting across the abyss — 49
5 'My house, my rules' — 58

The hardest things — **67**
6 Can we still win the war against tech? — 69
7 Things that go bump in the night — 81
8 Everyone in between — 92
9 'Let's talk about money, honey' — 105

When things seem bleak — **121**
10 The lonely child — 123
11 Danger and disaster — 135

Hopeful and helpful — **151**
12 Raising citizens to be proud of — 153
13 Do as you would be done by — 171
14 Best advice ever ... — 177

Useful resources — 193
Acknowledgements — 199
About the authors — 201

Introduction: It takes a Village

First, the good news: there is no single 'right' way to raise tweens, teens or young adults.

Relax.

The bad news? There's probably no way at *all* to raise tweens, teens or young adults and emerge unscathed.

But ... also relax! As parents, Karin and I have learnt this undeniable truth the hard way. By raising our own children, imperfectly, but also by closely observing, learning from and listening to almost 60 000 other parents (at the time of writing this book), who post daily on South Africa's most beloved online parenting community: The Village.

Raising children is a messy business. Parenting is a bold move and a feisty endeavour bursting with every catastrophe you swore to yourself (in those smug pre-parenting days,) that you would be the first parent in the history of parents not to suffer. The bad behaviour. The meltdowns. The disappointment. The anxiety. The sulks ... and that's just *us*!

It's not for nothing that, when parents first join our community, we promise unwavering support in the storms, an outstretched hand in the dark days and advice in the fog. Plus ... laughs. Because if we didn't laugh while attempting to raise our young, we would certainly turn to inappropriate sex, dangerous drugs and terrible behaviour ourselves.

But as challenging as parenting is, these family years are also the most precious in our lives. Looking back, from the other side of our children's teen years, those moments of raising them are often the most treasured times. Our golden moments – our happiest memories. Even though, of course, at the time it probably doesn't feel that way.

The trick? To find a way to enjoy our family time, love our children and believe in them through the thunder and lightning while navigating those stormy seas.

What is The Village?

The Village Online Community was launched seven years ago. Its ambition is to be a supportive forum of wisdom and care for families hoping for a better future for *all* our children.

The saying 'It takes a village to raise a child' is thought to originate from the Nigerian Igbo proverb *'oran a azu nwa'*, but similar proverbs and sentiments exist across the continent. From the moment The Village was launched, one fact has remained constant: raising families is easier when you are not alone. It takes a Village, after all.

And yet, communities of families are broken around the world. As we retreat behind screens and high walls, divorced, dysfunctional or simply alone, into our Netflixes and Uber deliveries and away from shared spaces, we seem to have lost that essential comforting magic and the natural, potent, healing and helping medicine of connection. Human beings are just better together.

We function best around a fire, under a tree, in multigenerational, diverse groups, watching other people's children, sharing our days and our thoughts; listening to each other's elders and learning from them; having our lives enriched by others' wisdom, insights and mistakes. Oh! Those invaluable, comforting, *funny* mistakes!

We cannot learn these invaluable lessons alone, from our sofas (or watch how someone else mucks it up so that you, in turn, can muck it up in your own unique way).

Introduction: It takes a Village

Or can we?

The Village created just this community online for the parents of teens, tweens and young adults. The content focuses on these age groups and the well-being of their parents. And over the years it has created its own strong magic. We have connection and care. And it works.

The most heartfelt thank you received by the admins of this Village is the most frequent one: 'I no longer feel so alone.' How can any parent feel alone when they have 60 000 others, in the same position, gathered together, ready to share and answer any question without judgement, cruelty or unkindness? What a bounty of information and advice we have gathered over the past seven years: the distilled wisdom, honest experience and voices of *so* many families, shared without artifice or competition, received without judgement or argument. Now, we hope to offer a compilation of all this advice in an even more valuable resource – a book.

In gathering seven years of online content and 60 000 voices into book form, we cannot promise that we have created an infallible guide. There is no such thing. But as we've mined the content and revisited the jewels from so many parents, what we have found are remedies and suggestions which, we hope, will provide authentic support to enable any reader to raise their family their own perfectly imperfect way.

We share advice from the real parenting experts (the parents themselves) in the hope that it will offer pause for thought, a fresh perspective or a valuable insight into a problem that our readers may be facing today. After all, no one is the first, nor the last, parent to toss and turn, late at night, wondering if their child (and they) will ever survive the roller coaster/storm/shit show of their tween, teen or young adult years.

Are you parenting a tween, teen or young adult? Buckle up, Buttercup! It's going to be a bumpy ride. There's no other path to adulthood, for all concerned. It is the zig and the zag, the long and winding road, the hellishly challenging but glorious parenting path. It must be done, but cutting the umbilical cord hurts both the mother and the child. The empty nest is a lonely and heartsore place.

When you get that call to the head teacher's office? When the school acceptances don't come? When the teenage door slams and you hear your darling child sobbing behind it? All awful. And calling an unanswered phone at 2 a.m. is the worst place in the world for any parent to be.

It is hard. We know.

But darkness only lasts till dawn. And with the valuable strategies outlined here from so many caring humans, you will survive. Your children will! And your family, we sincerely hope, will thrive.

It takes *The* Village and you have that help and connection, now, in your hands.

Some pointers about this book

C hildren do not come with a guidebook. Teenagers are not delivered with a pack of sedatives for each of their parents (although, of course, they should be). So, it is important to understand that this is no guidebook! Where parenting is involved, this book is no master plan. Your own parents will tell you – laughing hysterically perhaps, while reaching for a stiff G&T – that there never was a master plan.

Which perfect parents among us have not desperately and frequently wished for help along the way? None of us? *Exactly.*

What we parents need are the insights and lessons learnt of fellow travellers. We need advice, shared experiences and honesty. And these are here, in this book. We like to think it's a parenting book like no other. It's not written by experts, psychologists or gurus. It's written by 60 000 plus humans. Humans who are a bit battered and bruised, but still beautiful ... parents.

It's also written and curated by two people who, through fresh eyes (Karin) and total immersion (Vanessa), have observed the special magic of The Village, South Africa's most beloved parenting group, at work. Why magic? Because when we're in need, sometimes we don't want to be told what to do. What we need more than anything is other parents' experiences and lessons. This exposure is the powerful secret sauce of what we all need to get through these humbling years in one piece (never mind getting our children through in one piece). Thanks to The Village, we now know the value of advice shared with open hearts, good intentions and the desire to help. We have watched what happens when that help is received with open minds.

So, here's how to read this book: dip in, dip out. Not every piece of advice will resonate. Not every person's way will be your way. That's okay. The beauty of many voices is that, through gathering a picture of the community, you can find *your* place in it. As you read, you'll find the nuggets that help and resonate with *you*. You'll discover voices with which you identify. The most common comment we read from members of The Village is, 'I no longer feel alone.'

There is so much advice on The Village Facebook group – from insurance and holidays to hair removal and air fryers – that we had to narrow things down. So we focused on advice that has to do with parenting teens, which is the reason for the Facebook group's existence, and we narrowed things down some more by grouping the types of issues that come up repeatedly: safety, sex, money struggles, culture clashes, belief-system friction and intergenerational conflicts that represent entirely different world views.

The Village ethos accepts that our teens will drink/have sex/break the rules no matter how hard we try to steer them away from what we think of as dangerous and towards the safety of the straight and narrow. The Village ethos is also non-judgement and tolerance.

We don't want our or your kids to feel compromised by our interaction on The Village so all quotes have been chosen to reflect the wisdom and kindness of the stranger-friends we all are – and we thank all of you who allowed your names to be used. If your name wasn't used, it wasn't because your contributions haven't had value. We just had a *lot* to get through! Where we felt that a contributor's family could feel embarrassed or uncomfortable about their contribution, we have kept that contribution anonymous.

We have reproduced your quotes exactly as they are online with all their hurried typos, their casual grammar and their emojis. Your voices, exactly as they come to us from our Facebook page, are what we wanted to reflect here.

Now and again, we have stuck our heads around the door to give our own two cents' worth. Those bits are indicated by *Vanessa says* and *Karin says*.

There are a few useful resources that Villagers have recommended over the years tucked in at the back.

We hope you will find the collective wisdom of The Village as inspiring as we did when we were trawling through years and years and pages of pages of posts and comments to present you with your own best of The Village collection.

Read this book with an open mind. Read the chapters you need to, or devour it whole. Pull out your highlighter and your stickies – we guarantee you'll want to use them.

Please talk about the advice shared and stories told with your family and friends IRL. (Chances are, their advice and yours appears here, too!) Open minds and honest sharing are the most powerful tools any parent can have. Your Village is here!

With love and respect,
Vanessa and Karin

Talking about TALKING

Chapter 1

IT STARTS WITH *YOU* (AND US!)

There is no doubt that South Africa is a very tough place indeed in which to raise a happy family. Uncertainty, inequality, crime, lack of respect for, and trust in, leadership and government, corruption, collapse of institutions and infrastructure ... a toxic brew in which to expect an adult to thrive, and an equally challenging environment in which to marinate a child.

Most South African children do not have the opportunities we dream the rest of the world could offer them. But considering the reality of life in the rest of the world, things there aren't so rose-coloured either. And the grass isn't as green 'over there' as we dream it to be.

The relatively peaceful, predictable and optimistic years of the 1990s and early 2000s, when many of us were the age of our own children now, have long since been in our rear-view mirror. The global disaster of COVID has blown through and past. But it hit our children harder and more cruelly, research says, than any other group, apart from the elderly. The price South African families have paid, from a financial, social and mental health perspective, now overlays our country's problems, making things extremely challenging for most of us.

Today we are force-fed major challenges 24/7 due to our exposure to media. Climate change, global fractiousness, polarisation, war and even AI loom over us. Our children have inherited a fear-filled world. Life *everywhere* on our dust bowl is hard, angry, fast, competitive and uncertain.

But! You could say that a tough world is the perfect world for a South African. The future, whether here or abroad, is going to favour the brave, the courageous and the robust. Which many of us Saffers are: our history and circumstances mean we have had to be.

We have not been cushioned by the privilege of growing up in a robust, supportive economy. We have had to carry the shame and wound of our past and the disappointment of the present. We've had to make do with less and make it work. We've had to be adaptable and ingenious.

A successful South African's superpower is being born and bred tough. Born ready. Born to any challenge. We are the nation of 'Fok voort!' Of 'Maak 'n plan!' And most importantly, of ubuntu.

We have warm hearts and pirate spirits. Like our rugby team, we are hardcore. Not always the gentlest, the most cultured or the most sophisticated – but we are still strong and resourceful. We bounce back. We box above our weight. Of course, we are also battered and bruised. But we can, and *do*, succeed all over the world. And we succeed, against the odds, at home.

How do we pull off this success, against the odds?

If our abiding challenge is how to thrive and grow here, our secret sauce is making the best of what we have, turning hardship to our advantage or at least coming up with a successful means of coping.

What can make one child a survivor and another a tragic statistic? The first part of the answer: it takes one adult. Remember this quote by American motivational speaker, Josh Shipp? 'Every kid is one caring adult away from being a success story.' It only takes one adult to give a child the positivity, self-belief and optimism to cope with what any country can throw at them.

As a parent, being that adult is the greatest challenge and responsibility any of us will be given in our lifetime.

If one parent or responsible adult is okay, the family can be okay. And in tough times, for every family it is essential that one person, one adult, role models that. We are uncertain and untrusting about the future. We've been hurt by our past, it's true. But successful parents have coping mechanisms to ensure that they do not pass this negativity down to their children.

If a child witnesses only unhappiness, fear and defeat, they will learn to be defeated, fearful and unhappy. But if we dig into our essential South African superpowers – that superb resilience, hardiness, warmth and great sense of humour – we'll find we have all it takes to be the parent our children need. We can do it. We *do* do it. Your child's success starts with *you*.

The second part of the answer: a strong adult knows it's okay to ask for help. Just as it takes one adult in each family to be okay, it takes a Village to support, help, inspire and advise that adult. We asked The Village for their advice on how to raise a resilient child in a hard country and an unfair world. These are some of the answers:

Be a good example

As **Hayley Reichert** said, 'Children watch and learn from your actions far more than your words. If you're consistently showing up for yourself and your family, focusing on positive thinking and solutions rather than just seeing problems, they'll learn how to think and act with grit'.

'Walk the walk. Talk the talk. Instil and create strong foundations and inner confidence. Encourage thinking and creativity,' said **Stephanie Day**.

Anette Corder expanded on this idea: 'We as parents try consciously to focus on the good and the beautiful. Sometimes one must dig just a little deeper. We try to live by example. We greet everyone that we pass by. We acknowledge and thank serve providers. We greet and chat to neighbours. We communicate and dialogue intentionally with each other. We make time for each other. I believe this is where it starts. In the home. We try and see challenges as life lessons to be learned. We are still here, and focus heavily on the beauty and kindness around us. Daily. We journal, mostly with gratitude. We create. We listen to beautiful music. We are extra kind to unkind and hurting people. It begins with a smile. Am following this with gratitude.'

'We show them by example,' says **Belinda Mutti Smith**. 'Every minute of every day South Africans adapt, adjust, plan and get on with it because we have to. Nothing in life is guaranteed, regardless of where you are living. Our children aren't protected from the tough stuff. They learn how to be conscious role players in their own futures and advocate for what should be. They are exposed to different voices and truths and have to learn to witness and work with it all. That's a gift for a global citizen!'

Be positive

'Surround yourself with positive (young) people. Avoid the old farts,' said **Lynda Van Zyl**. 'You'll be amazed how contagious optimism and positivity can be. Look how Brett Lindeque, "The Good Things Guy", took a small idea and it caught fire. Luckily young people are naturally optimistic and idealistic (yes and often naive) but we can learn a lot from them. It's a great survival strategy.'

Gavin Fish believes that 'Schools and parents need to be so much more closely intertwined. Our teens must have opportunities to discover and explore their strengths (what they are innately good at), to identify their passions (that which blows their hair back), and to then ask where society most needs their unique blend of strengths and passions. It is not a perfect equation, circumstances differ, but it does help with a sense of purpose and optimism.'

'Honestly, I think that just by living here, in this country, in this time, we instill that optimism every day,' offered **Kim Penstone**.

'I'm not saying we don't get frustrated by the loadshedding, or mad with lawless driving. But we are forever "making a plan", "vokking maar voord", laughing at ourselves and the weird old country in which we live. We model resilience and optimism every day in this country. In so many different ways. And our kids see it.'

Anina Potgieter also recommends being positive: 'There is no perfect other country to live in. Contribute to solve our problems – don't just complain. South Africa has an energy like very few other places. Be grateful for what we have and give back to communities and people in need around us.'

Which neatly brings us to …

Look for the good

Gillian Freimond Rightford believes that 'As much bad as there is, there's more good. Teach them to look for the good'.

This idea was expanded on by admin **Ann Ellis Brown**, who quoted American broadcaster Fred Rogers as saying, 'When I was a boy and I would see scary things in the news, my mother would say to me, "Look for the helpers. You will always find people who are helping." To this day, especially in times of disaster, I remember my mother's words, and I am always comforted by realising that there are still so many helpers – so many caring people in this world'. Ann continued, 'This quote inspired me. I am SO proud of the countless South Africans who drop what they're doing and help when it's needed. I'd add that, as adults and parents, we shouldn't just look for the helpers … we should BE the helpers (or at least actively support them) as an example to our kids'.

Keep things in perspective

Cindy Naude asked her eldest what he has taken to heart over the years of living here. She posted his response: 'Always remember that though life truly sucks at times, someone longs for the life you are living and would swap without blinking an eye. So get up and get over yourself ☺ ☺'

He also offered his four guiding lights:

1. '**Gratitude:** Stop and take stock of all the blessings you have or things you don't have to deal with, and learn to look for the things in your life to be thankful for.
2. **Hope:** [You might be] struggling ... now. But it's not always going to be this way. You alive? Heart beating? Good, then it's not too late to change your circumstances.
3. **Kindness:** It costs nothing. Don't be an ass 🍑
4. Last but not least ... if you are ever at a crossroads, **always choose to do the hard things**. That's where character gets built.'

'I think a good start is to admit that, whilst not undermining the severity, injustice and violence inherent in ours, every country appears to have problems,' wrote **Chantal Hefferman MacKenzie**. 'The UK is a mess, most of Europe has a refugee crisis, the States ... need I say more? Yes our youth are subjected to daily doses of difficulty, prejudice and unfairness, and sadly the norm is almost to nudge them off African soil, but fortunately thanks to modern technology the world has become a smaller place, more accessible. We can WhatsApp and call without those eye-watering international call costs, share pictures in real time on various social media platforms and flights are way more affordable than they have ever been. Yes families are being forced to commute for visits, but it is do-able. I think we need to focus on that.'

'My message was mostly: Sometimes you are the pigeon, other times you are the statue!' wrote **Debbie Engelbrecht**. 'The biggest message I tried to convey is that when life is not giving us what we want, we just need to remember why we were born with good heads on us! Simply use them to the best of our ability. Nobody can ever ask more than that from you. Also in every bit of chaos there is an opportunity to make a difference.'

Sherry Walklett posted the following: 'I think we start with unconditional love. Then over time, and as they grow up, we have lots of conversations around what kindness is versus bullying. Around how fortunate our children are in comparison to others. Have the conversation around how life can be difficult but with enough resilience, they can tackle anything. Let them understand that they won't always get what they want but that this should never stop them from trying. Also, reminding them of how proud you are of them and that you think they are exceptional little humans who will grow up into exceptional adults. I mostly raised my brother and sister and I remember having just such conversations with them. I now have the same with my youngest nephew.'

Encourage grit and resilience

'Equip them with regulatory skills or ways to release anxiety, stress and tension. Whether it's spiritual and emotional (like deep breathing, meditation) or finding an outlet like surfing, hiking, being present in nature. Living here has multiple layers of stress and uncertainty, and not to mention the hardship and negativity in the news all around us. To be resilient and succeed here you need to draw deeply on your own reserves,' wrote **Anita Nesbit**.

But also, as **Catherine Donaldson** says, we must 'allow our children to make mistakes. Allow them to "fail". Do not rush in to fix everything for them. If they never face adversity etc. they can never learn resilience. If they don't fall, they won't learn how to get up. If they don't face disappointment, they will struggle later. Taking ownership of their responsibilities is crucial.'

Lesley Scott, one of The Village admin team, unpacked all these themes: 'I think we have always lived in a world where, except for a lucky few, things do not always turn out for the best and life can be disappointing.

'We raise optimists by instilling a spirit of curiosity in our kids;

we need to encourage them to explore their world and learn to trust their own instincts when it comes to safety and risk. We need to find and point out the good things that happen, and the good people around us, often the things we forget to notice. Cultivate the spirit of Ubuntu – I am because You are. We (as adults) need to become more socially responsible and responsive, and make those small changes for the better where we can, and we need to teach our kids to do the same – although I think they often already do.

'Our generation (worldwide) is considered one of the most entrepreneurial and innovative, and a lot of that is attributed to the fact that we were not mollycoddled or helicoptered or lawn-mowered. We instil bravery but swallowing down our own fears, and letting our kids figure things out for themselves, knowing that we are nearby if they need us, but letting them try, and maybe fail, or maybe make a plan on their own.

'I compare resilience to a scar – it often comes after a wound. I would rather encourage grit – or determination. Grit is considered the biggest factor in determining success. Can you get up after a fall or bounce back after a setback? Grit is built by building self-confidence, self-belief, self-awareness, self-understanding and self-worth.

'One thing we don't all have though is the easy ability to be accepting and inclusive, because we (SA) grew up in an intolerant and divided society. This is a mindset that I believe we all have to challenge every day, so that we can intentionally alter our ingrained and often unconscious ways of thinking. We need to model this way of being to our kids – always asking "why do I think/feel/behave this way?" This is how we build compassion.

'The world is not and has never been an easy place to live and many adults see their youth through rose-coloured glasses. But comparing the world of our youth to the world of today robs kids of the opportunity to believe that the present is exactly that – a gift.

'We have raised a generation of young people who on the whole are kinder, more tolerant, more aware, more inclusive and who have more opportunities than we ever did. As their parents, we must be realistic and speak to them about the fact that there will always be days where they may feel defeated or bitter or resentful but there will also be days where they will feel empowered and emboldened and grateful and joyful.

'Our grandparents went to war (some twice) to fight for a world that was free. Many of our parents, or even our spouses or partners also fought in wars – either because they were conscripted and had no choice, or because they were fighting for their very lives and freedoms. Our children (at least here in South Africa) are one of the very first generations in nearly 2 centuries not to have to go to war, and they have the power to keep it that way. By raising our kids to be active participants in our democracy (regardless of the state it's currently in), they hold the power and in turn the responsibility for the future of the country. The vote of the youth (under 25) is almost nonexistent, for many reasons. But that one X can be the most significant way in which they get to determine the country's future – and that seems like a pretty good reason to stick around in my book.'

How do we bolster *ourselves* in a wild, wild world?

The trite saying 'It is what it is' is both super-annoying and deeply Zen. It's like someone telling you to chill when you're either feeling chill or not at all chill – it can seem patronising and glib.

But when you can access calm (a true parental superpower!), you can move on from the challenge of our reality and make it work for you – 'calm' meaning not showing or feeling nervousness or other strong emotions.

It is a severely underrated parental skill and yet an essential one. If we understand and accept that parenting is messy and sore, that it's going to be a long and bumpy flight, we may find ourselves intentionally being calmer as we face the storms that will no doubt come our way – and brace for them.

That is the parental position, especially when raising teens and tweens and young adults: braced. As solid as we can be.

We have to take that stance. We really have to. As a parent, our options for checking out are limited by our responsibilities. With some help, a deep breath and some luck, most of us do cope!

The oxygen on the plane: If you're nice to everyone but unkind to yourself ...

- 'You cannot pour from an empty cup. Please reach out to someone you trust. Many of us deal with feelings of being overwhelmed by life and all the balls we are trying to keep in the air. I once read a story about the balls we juggle: kids, spouse, work etc. Some of the balls are glass (the ones most precious to us), while others are rubber. It's okay to let the rubber balls bounce sometimes. We can't be everything to everyone.' – **Lesley Scott**
- 'Forgive yourself for not getting it all right all the time. Imagine if you were your own daughter, would you judge her, as you are judging yourself? Would you expect your best friend to be perfect? Don't expect perfection from yourself ... Let people who love you help you.' – **Roxane Litchia**
- 'It's time to answer the question, if you are trying to be everything to everyone else, [what] do you want to be to yourself? The best option you have is attitude to gratitude right now! What are you doing to feel gratitude every day? Wake up in the morning and write down 3 things you see that you are grateful for. Then read them out loud!! You forgot how grateful you are by lashing out with overwhelmed anger at yourself. This is a trauma release reaction. Take time to breathe slow and deep each time you feel like you want to pop – just stop ... and take a breath. You are a wonderful and resourceful mother and warrior woman. You wouldn't call out for support if you didn't care. You have a bucket full of gratitude for your beautiful family, time

to acknowledge and take ownership and give yourself the love you deserve. When you give out love to yourself too, so you shall receive love. You have the support, you are not alone. Hugs and love.' – **Avra Poelmann**

- 'You cannot be the wife, mom, employee, daughter, etc. if your wheels are falling off. If you can take a step back before those wheels fall, please try. It sounds trite but it's true. Stop trying to be who everyone else expects. Stop trying to be the so-called perfect anyone. Just be there for yourself. And once you get you ok the rest will fall into place with boundaries. You can do it. Be kindest to you first. If you can't do that then you can't do it for anyone else.' – **Catherine Donaldson**
- 'The first thing you need to do is stop caring so much about what people think and start taking one small step at a time. You need to learn to love yourself and give yourself a break. The only person who expects you to be perfect is you. Seriously, we put such unnecessary pressure on ourselves.' – **Monique Storm Slater**
- 'Hang on a second. I hear how you are solely responsible for an entire universe here. So while you are looking after everyone, who is looking after you? Sounds a little bit unfair to me. I think you should take a break and breathe. Discuss how you feel with your family. They need to pitch in and help. They can't possibly expect you to make it easier for all of them at your own expense.' – **Charlene Radyn**

What does being kind to yourself even mean?

It means give yourself a break. Things can be hard, and life is demanding. Don't make it worse by trash-talking yourself, is what it means.

If you stop being rude to yourself in your head, you won't necessarily solve your problems, but it's easier to concentrate on a marathon when there isn't someone on the sidelines telling you that you suck.

You wouldn't say 'idiot' or 'stupid' to your kids when they make a mistake, so why is it okay to say it to yourself?

Melanie Loebenberg Novitzkas holds up a mirror for us all to look into:

'I really try and be kind and conscious of not being an arsehole. And then I told someone who was desperately looking for a job they were unemployable. The person whose confidence was way down and who was being so deliberate in applying.

'I was also impatient and not very nice to someone whose last child had just moved out. She felt so very sad about this loss and I berated her and dismissed her grief. Horrible right? Like proper mean girl.

'The person I told all this to ... is *me*. Why are we super nice to other people and then awful to ourselves? Then because I am generally quite self-aware I had to be a little harsh that I was so awful to myself.

'I am sorry. I am going to try and treat myself the way I treat my friends and kids. I am going to use this flood of maternal feelings I have about my kids leaving home to mother myself. And I know I am employable. Of course I do.

'So stop telling yourself you are lazy or fat or ugly or old or unlovable or useless or a bad mother or can't get work or all the other crap you say that's unkind and you would never say to another. We really need some gentle self-love.'

Being kind to yourself also means taking control of what you can and recognising what you *don't* have control over.

- You don't have control over the rising food prices, but you do have control of food wastage at home.
- You don't have control over what people ask you to do, but you do have control over what you will and won't say yes to.
- You don't have control over the stress that you and your family will be exposed to in the normal workings of life, but you do have control over whether the coping mechanisms you choose will make your life less or more manageable.
- You also don't have control over what people think of you and

your life and your body and the way you parent and your style, but you have control over how much you care about what other people think.

Routines, non-negotiables, spreadsheets, boundaries and planning are also ways of being kind to yourself. Facing things instead of running away from them is another way. One Villager shared a quote that self-care wasn't about bubble baths and cake but about building a life you don't always want to escape from.

No one is going to tell you, the adult, when you've taken on enough or are doing too much. Setting the limits on how much you can bear or fit in is your main job. It's like the thing about being in an aeroplane and putting your own mask on first so that you don't pass out before you can help smaller people put theirs on.

The task of setting boundaries and making rules is an ongoing one too. Just because you vowed to always bake a cake for your mother's birthday, it doesn't mean five years on that this is sustainable.

If people are treating you badly, remind yourself of what Villager **Wendy Bowyer von Blerk** said: 'People will always treat us the way we keep allowing them to treat us.'

Circumstances change, life changes. Kids are constantly changing – they suddenly eat tomatoes, the person they once hated is now their best friend, they decide to give up first-team hockey, they become the best at something or the worst at something, and they go from saying nothing for days to talking non-stop for two hours.

We, meanwhile, are getting older, more irritable, a bit chubbier, more relaxed, poorer, richer, wiser, happier, divorced, more disciplined, freer from expectation and more tattooed. We're becoming exercise monsters or people who no longer use exercise as a way to seek perfection. We grow up eating meat, and then decide to stop. We finally have the courage to live openly queer, stop helping our abusive parents to abuse us, or give up on romance and focus on growing cabbage.

Everything, everywhere, all the time, is changing and we cope! We adapt. We flow along.

Sometimes being kind to ourselves is nothing more than reminding ourselves that things change, and we need to change alongside them. Instead of shouting at ourselves, we need to be kind.

Villager **Carmen Andries** once wrote: 'People are going through the most, and it's tough. Many just reach out for an encouraging word and some form of validation. Kindness makes every situation less threatening and chaotic.'

She went on to talk about her 24-year-old daughter who has a progressive illness. 'I never planned this for my life, neither for her life. We had other plans. However, we adjust and make it work. Every day, we just show up and take it ONE DAY AT A TIME. Let's be kind, let's spread kindness. It takes a Village.'

It also takes a self to be kind to a self. No one is coming to save you from loadshedding or ADHD or burnout or yourself. So make sure you're more than okay and – when things are not overwhelming – make sure you find ways to plug into the joy of being a social human surrounded by people who are more good than bad.

Responding to a Villager's frightening story of an airport run that went badly wrong and could have been much worse had it not been for the gentle Metro police and for other drivers who stopped and helped her, **Diane Hill** wrote, 'So grateful you are both ok and secondly that your faith in human nature is restored. It's easy to calibrate down to negativity and drama, so when we get reminded that actually most of the world are decent people who want to support, love and connect, we have the opportunity to remind ourselves that it's not all bad'.

Be kind to others? How, even?

If you don't want to be judged all the time on your failings, *a good way to stop caring is to stop judging*. If you're constantly judging others all the time for their perceived failures, you will imagine that everyone is like you, thinking about all the ways you fail.

Stop it. What others think of you is none of your business.

How to be kind to one another

Here's some excellent advice from Villager **Mpho Makoko**: 'I lost my dad a few years ago. Tragic and painful. I was 22. A friend of mine lost both her parents through a murder/suicide when she was 1.

'Whilst we both grieve for what could have been, I understand that her grief is different to mine. Her loss is different and the complex feelings brought by the loss of her parents as a baby is different to mine. Not better, or worse – but different.

'It really broke my heart when a young widow had to explain herself on why she wanted to find people that have experienced a loss similar to hers to navigate this journey. In no way had she said that anyone else's grief is less.

'One of the things I have learnt in my adult life and interactions on social media is to "talk" to myself when I feel the urge to reply to someone, particularly someone going through a difficult time.

'Three things are important to me:
1. Will what I say leave this person in a "better" position than before they read my opinion?
2. Is it kind (even if it's an alternative opinion)?
3. Have I steered away from allowing my opinion to be clouded by my own misjudgements and taken the time to think what it is like to be in this person's shoes?

'So often we rush to reply, to defend ourselves and our experiences even when we are not being attacked. We project, we show no sympathy – in instances where we should have ignored and been silent. These days we turn everything into some kind of competition, grief-olympics, parenting olympics etc. etc. "Oh, she said she liked a banana – that means she hates oranges" type of situation.

'I hope that I am able to continue to be a comfort to my friend; that on Father's Day when she looks at photos of me and my dad just before I went to university – and thinks of all the milestones I had with him that she never had with both her parents – that I do not turn that into some kind of competition, because we are both grieving and we always will but the truth is, realistically, I have a lot more to hold on to than she ever will! Acknowledging that does not mean I am not in pain over the loss of my dad.'

Let them

Have you heard of the 'Let them' theory? Some Villagers heard about it for the first time on The Village when someone posted a link to podcaster Mel Robbins explaining it. It's where, if someone does something differently from the way you would have done it, you say 'let them' to yourself. Instead of getting cross or worried or judgemental, just shrug your shoulders and let them get on with it.

This is probably more important in parenting than anywhere else. We have to find that line between helping our teens and letting them figure things out for themselves. And if they have a way of doing things that doesn't align exactly with the way you would do it, try to 'let them' as often as you can (as long as it doesn't disrupt the home and family).

It saves a lot of energy to just let people be who and do what they want to be and do. That it's not your way of being and doing doesn't make it wrong. What's wrong is tying yourself up in knots because of how other people do things.

It's worse for you than it is for them. So: let them.

Chapter 2

HELP!
WHO IS THIS ALIEN?

At about midnight one day, an anonymous poster sent up a distress flare, punctuated by many exclamation points: 'No, please don't tell me I have to wait till she is 25 for the frontal cortex to develop!!! That's ten years to go!! Needing some support here, Villagers!!! I can't be the punching bag for 10 more years!! Help!!'

There comes a time when every parent has to face the extremely humbling truth: you and your offspring are *not* the unicorn family who are going to dodge the wrecking ball wrought by the onslaught of adolescence.

Their adolescence humbles *all* of us.

Parents may intellectually know (or have been told by our older, battle-wearier brothers, sisters, older parents, any other Breeder, clinging to each other for dear life around the football field) what lies ahead of us. But, like those very parents before us, we hoped, secretly *believed*, that we would be the exception.

Listen in to a parent's internal monologue (before their child's adolescence): 'Phew. Finally, post-baby, toddler and pre-school years. Finally free to have a drink at 5 p.m. on a Sunday night! Look at us! WOOHOO! *Not* awake watching *Barney & Friends* at 5 a.m. on a weekend! WINNING!'

Maybe that parent is feeling the luxury of pride and self-congratulation: 'Phew! He/she/they have found their way through primary school and it's been ... terrific! Don't like to boast, but they've been voted captain of their house, captain of their rugby team! *And* they got a 7 in Maths!'

Observe the pre-adolescent child's behaviour: He/she/they are affectionate to their adult. Chatty in the back of the car. Cute. Obedient. Yes, will play with kid from down the road, if bribed. Listens to, and obeys, strongly worded threats about putting down devices, putting out lights. No vapes. No porn on their hand-me-down cell phone. No drugs. No friends vomiting on the soft furnishings.

Complacent parents of pre-adolescent sweetie pies, stand back! The show is about to begin!

Parent in child's mid-adolescence: 'OMG. Help! SOS. WTAF happened here?' 'Pass me a drink. No, make that a double. Okay, twist my arm, make it a treble. Keep it coming.' (Loads several distress posts on The Village.)

Kid in mid-adolescence: 'You're all lame. I hate you. My friends hate me. I hate myself. You don't understand. Go away.' (Door slams. Sobs. Or worse: silence.)

And that's just the start.

Things other parents may (but psychologists may not) remind you about when your child:

- At best, turns from moppet into sulky, stroppy, smelly stranger
- *Really* seems to go off the rails. (Strength. We're here to help you with that.)

Tweens, teens and young adults are entirely under the control of the adults in their lives. And yet, every adolescent is just trying to grow into themselves. Often, the early signals of those selves emerge at adolescence and are worrying to us, their parents. What we start to see might be a self that is challenging to our beliefs, our culture, our religion, our values, our expectations. We worry that what's emerging may not lead our children to success and happiness.

In our attempts to guide or protect our children – which, if we're honest, are probably attempts to wrangle them into being versions of ourselves – we can stifle them by denying them the freedom to challenge us. They may struggle to grow into themselves while they're dependent on, and yet in some way in conflict with, us. This emergence of a self is hard for them to figure out, and simultaneously a challenge to parental expectations: it can create a bumpy ride as parent and child learn to accept each other's individuality. At worst, it can result in a breakdown of the relationship.

Food for thought: the bad and perplexing behaviour we think we experience from them may just be a reaction to our behaviour.

Our Villager from the start of this chapter knows why this strange and awful transformation is happening. Whereas pleasing you was once their main instinctive survival drive, there are other things driving and affecting their behaviour now:

- **The normal and necessary second severing of the umbilical cord.** Adolescents are programmed to start separating from the family and finding their own (eventually beautiful) adult selves.
- **The prefrontal cortex is still developing.** This is the part of the brain that regulates behaviour and emotions: it's responsible for skills like planning and prioritising; it's the part of the brain we use for making good decisions; and it's where good judgement happens because it's where we weigh up consequences ... once we're in our mid-20s. Unfortunately, it's a slow starter, one of the last parts of the brain to mature. And while the brain is fine-tuning itself, our teens are entering a phase of risk-taking. They do not have access to the kind of forethought and emotional control that adults have. (Or should have. Dealing with a teenager can sometimes bring out the teenager in us too.)

- **Tweens and teens still take many of their cues for navigating their social life from TV series.** Fights, misunderstandings, nastiness and every other social ill they face in their own untelevised lives are not resolved in 28 minutes. When this doesn't happen in real life, it causes frustration, falling outs, confusion, fear and anger. Thanks, Disney Channel. Real life is nothing like a sitcom.
- **Tweens and teens have taken their cues for how they should look from Instagram and TikTok.** An unhappy, badly behaved child is a child struggling to love their own, incomplete project. Learning to accept and celebrate yourself while thumbing through filtered clips of influencers, trying to be kind to yourself when you live in a world of comparison, is hard – even for adults. Tweens and teens are spotty, gawky and weighed down with baby fat. They have teeth not yet corrected by expensive and embarrassing orthodontics. They have breasts bursting out of trainer bras and periods that sometimes arrive mortifyingly unexpectedly. They have hairy legs and squeaky voices. They know this. Tweens, particularly, spend hours scrutinising themselves more cruelly and critically than we can imagine. Tweens and teens wish – or rather, *need* – to fit in, to disappear into the safety of conformity and yet still be chosen to be 'popular'. Tweens' and teens' social lives are puzzles that are extremely hard to complete.
- **Fear of cancellation and the risk of public shaming.** In a world where words and behaviours are more policed than ever and mistakes can result in 'cancellation', where feelings are raw and connections are complicated and charged with risk and danger, our children walk a tightrope of suppressed and fearful behaviour in their peer groups and schools. This awakening to the urgent necessity to adapt the way we talk and behave, to remove the words and behaviours that have marginalised and diminished groups of people before, is essential progress.

But making mistakes has never been more perilous. This country today is a dangerous place to be trying to find and mould yourself into an adult. Social media ups the jeopardy of public shame and disgrace. Everyone knows everything. Children may behave worse at home as it is their only 'safe' space: if home doesn't feel like a safe space, the behaviour, the distress and the consequences are even worse.

- **The youth are lonely.** Thanks to broken connections due to the pandemic, social media, lack of safety, freedom, homeschooling ... teenagers are the second-loneliest group of people alive, according to sources like Scott Galloway's podcasts. When teenagers and young adults are meant to be testing their wings by switching from home to social lives, from family to friends, becoming more socially independent from their parents, this generation faces uncertainty. The more privileged do not have the same freedom that many previous generations had. The less privileged have no certainty of a path ahead. Competition is fierce for places in schools and universities, for jobs. 'Good behaviour' is often a 'symptom' of confidence and security – which is currently in short supply.
- **Tweens and teens can experience social alienation and exclusion.** They may feel inadequate, unwanted and unpopular (very sore and serious emotions in the young), as peers they may have considered friends post about activities on social media from which they may have been excluded. Where is it safe for this child to rage and punish? Home. That's where.
- And then the most obvious and least terrifying reason of all: **tweens and teens are awash with hormones.** They are irritable. They are uncomfortable. They think they look horrible. And they are suddenly allergic to their adults. Not dissimilar to many of their parents, who are often inconveniently neck-deep in menopause when adolescence strikes!

Lessons from The Village: You are not alone

'One day the alien leaves I'm told and they become your best friend. In the meantime we are all just winging it. Strongs Mommy 🤍' – **Andrea Van Geems Penrose**

'A teenager's brain is still under development. I am patiently waiting for that prefrontal cortex to be properly developed so that I can get a proper conversation out of one of my kids. Until then, I have to cope with their moods and grunts. My daughter had a total meltdown this morning, but then came home and cleaned her room. That was enough apology for me.' – **Barbara Meyer**, in a thread about teaching teenagers how to apologise properly

'Why can't you sometimes, when you've had it up to here with the bad attitude, respond with "For fuck's sake, you are not the only person in the world shit things have happened to"?' – **Anonymous** (Half the responders said, 'Because that's not cool and it invalidates your child's experience.' The other half said, 'Yup, I've also dropped the odd f-bomb.')

'At what age do boys stop challenging their moms about everything you say, ask, comment on or basically every subject you try to converse about? I'm hanging in there but it feels like a very thin thread. Is there a date and time? I miss my sweet little boy!!!' – **Anonymous**

Another Villager posted a picture of a door frame without a door. Sick of her daughter's door slamming despite her repeated requests for her to stop slamming it, she took the door off the hinges when her daughter was out one day.

They are desperate times, these teen years. For them, of course, but also for us. Ten truckloads of understanding about the teenage brain, the patience of all the saints put together and screaming into a pillow will probably not get us through them without our questioning where we went wrong.

The Village is the quintessential place to go for a scream into the void when your teenager becomes monstrous. Most of the other parents' responses remind The Villagers that the changes in behaviour start with us, the parents. For example, when one Villager was getting to the point at which they wanted to throw something against a wall, **Kika Magalhaes** offered this advice: 'Pace yourself, breathe deeply and have awesome girlfriends.'

But yes, while they are changing, we have to change too. And that includes the way we discipline.

The D-word

One of the original founders of The Village is psychologist Megan de Beyer. In her excellent book, *How to Raise a Man: The Modern Mother's Guide to Parenting Her Teenage Son*, Megan points out that the way we parented our toddlers is not going to work with our teens. Authoritative (not authoritarian) parenting was absolutely the correct way to lay a good foundation when disagreements may have been about brushing teeth. But when it comes to the D-word – discipline – with teens, there are better ways of managing their behaviour than by creating a dictatorship in which everyone is unhappy.

There are good reasons for keeping connections open, and you can't do that if you're still trying to rule your roost with the proverbial rod of iron.

In the early days of The Village, **Kate Gerber Furmie** noted that in an overly strict household, teens tend to fall into three groups: the Ones Who Fall In Line, the Bucking Broncos and the Ones Who Withdraw.

The Ones Who Fall In Line are easy care. They follow the rules. There are no surprises. They perform optimally within the structure you've carefully formed for the household.

The Bucking Broncos rage against the establishment. Everything is stupid, everything is wrong. You don't understand. They hate you.

The Ones Who Withdraw are secretive. They lock you out of their lives. You don't know where they are or what they're up to. You have to question everything they tell you.

But the thing that all three types have in common is fear.

The first group may seem like they're doing well, that they're no trouble at all, but they are still fearful of carving out a sense of self. They are afraid to step out of line and establish a self-sustaining identity. They will usually be slightly codependent, always trying to fill the needs of, and seek approval from, a parent. This does not bode well for future romantic relationships. A healthy person needs a developed sense of self with well-established boundaries. A teenager needs to be able to say, 'I respect that those are yours, but these are mine.'

The second group may be a rebellious nightmare (if only for a time). But they are fearful that they will fail you so, in anticipation of this, they have already told you to take a long walk off a short pier. They will desperately try to break free to establish a sense of self but may fall in with the wrong crowd because at the end of the day they still seek some sort of support, understanding and approval. It just may not be from you any longer.

The last group is so fearful of failure and the shame that comes with making a mistake in your eyes that it is easier to be deceitful than to risk your 'rejection'. With this breakdown in communication between parent and teenager comes the very real danger that your child will be exposed to hurts, to drugs and to people with an agenda – and that you will be none the wiser. Instead of rocking the boat at home, your child will try to cope without you. They will feel lost and alone despite being part of a functional and loving family.

I do not advocate for parents being 'friends' to their teenagers. Teenagers need a firm but fair disciplinarian to keep them on the right path. They need to see healthy relationships between family members to feel secure in themselves. One of these is the parent-to-child relationship. But you may need to develop a completely different approach to a teenager. They can no longer be as easily cajoled and controlled. They are forming their own personalities. As a parent, you need to show that blossoming personality respect and allow them more freedom – or risk them moving towards you in an unhealthy way or away from you in a hazardous way. Most importantly, a teenager must feel secure enough to come to you with anything, without fear of severe reprisals.

Things to think about when they're pushing all the buttons

Boundaries and consequences

'I was told by a psychologist that often we loosen the boundaries as our teens start pushing them. We should be tightening them and showering them with love. The tight boundaries and love showering fills up their cups.' – **Wendy Bowyer van Blerk**

'Aaah, you have arrived at that point where even on the days that you feel no love you must really like them alot 😉. Be firm about the really important boundaries and shower them with even more love. They actually want and need that love. You got this!' – **Affidha Shaikh Ebrahim**

It's not always about you

As **Kika Magalhaes** noted: 'This behaviour has absolutely nothing to do with you! Nothing! It has to do with them figuring out who they are. Specially amongst their peers. Any love you need isn't going to come from her but you need to continue loving her FIERCELY! You need to have awesome x-ray vision to know when things need to be unpacked and how. You are irrelevant for the next while! Just pace yourself and do things for yourself that feed your soul.

'Have music in your home, make it a haven for her, bake and let it smell nice, laugh 🤍'

BSS – Big Scary Stuff

When there doesn't seem to be a way out, The Village comes through. Like the time when a Villager posted this plea for support and help as her daughter hit Ground Zero:

'My husband and I don't have children together. We weren't able to conceive and he doesn't have children of his own. I just have one daughter.

'My [16-year-old] daughter has been extremely difficult for almost two years. We have had her with psychiatrists and psychologists. She starts arguing with me and after asking nicely far too many times I then sternly reprimand her and she gets so angry she starts punching the walls and shouting. She has threatened multiple times to commit suicide and cuts herself.

'She has always attended good schools and we offer her a loving stable home. My husband has provided everything for her since a baby and only wants the best for her. She treats him so terribly and looks at him with complete hatred. He has given up and our marriage is taking a lot of strain.

'My husband is the kindest, most giving person I have met and we believe we are each other's soul mates. We love each other dearly, however we can't live with this constant stress and conflict from my daughter.

'She left the house with her boyfriend this morning without telling us and we can't get hold of her so we have no idea if she is coming home.

'I am afraid there could be something mentally wrong with her or is this how teenagers generally are these days? I am desperate and feel so hopeless. '

In response, one of our Villagers shared her experience and what helped her family:

'Stay strong. We had a somewhat similar situation with our youngest son. [My husband is his] step dad. There were problems at school and general rebellion. Those were really tough years but they have now passed thankfully. When you are in the situation it feels never ending. A few things we did that helped us – not sure if they will work for you:

1. 'We never allowed our son to cause division between us; as parents we stuck together.

2. He knew that he could have a hard time, puberty, unhappiness and whatever else he had (there was a lot), but in our home there was one set of rules that applied to everyone. He was welcome to disagree with them but not allowed to disrespect. He also understood the consequences for disrespecting these. Those days were especially tough for me because my husband is strict and the consequences were always immediate – no excuses. As tough as this path was, it taught him boundaries, which he always pushed, but he knew there was a line not to be crossed.
3. We continued to show him love, making it clear that the only thing we had a problem with was his behaviour, not him.
4. We prayed for guidance and wisdom. He did go to boarding school but we took him out in Grade 11 when the behaviour did not improve and focused on helping him before we lost him. This was many years of ups and downs and when he was in matric the penny dropped and we could see improvements, which have continued.

'We also offered for him to see a psychologist which he refused until he was ready (last year only). Continue to love her but help her by setting those boundaries: unfortunately at this age there are so many things they are dealing with which can also be confusing. Out of all our kids he is the one who calls home the most to check on us and often jokes about some of the parenting challenges we had with him. To which I reply, it's too soon, then he just laughs. It does get better: consider seeing a psychologist to help you put together your plan and gain strength, you will need it. Don't forget to appreciate your husband for sticking with you, that is true love. I've always told my husband that if the roles were reversed and I was the step mom, I would have definitely divorced him because that is drama I did not sign up for, so grateful that he stuck it out. Sending you 🤍 and best wishes.'

Seqel Hall shared this insight: 'To me it sounds like something is wrong. Not WITH her but rather WITHIN her. She sounds like she's in pain. Unfortunately, due to the hectic world we live in and the realisation that the "good old ways" actually incite a lot more trauma in people than anything else, a loving and stable home isn't always enough. Teens these days are way more mature and are going through so much that you as a person probably didn't have to. She sounds like she feels alone. She sounds like she has trauma that needs dealing with. She sounds like she needs guidance. Not that you haven't offered that. But I don't think a boarding school would be a solution. Love and patience and guidance 🩶 Don't give up on her.'

Jane Bradpiece Plit, therapist and longtime Villager added: 'Keep breathing, in most cases, they are their worst selves with you because:

1. you are (should be) their safe space to be their worst selves, without losing your love
2. they need to establish an individual, independent identity
3. it will pass, most likely, and one day, as fast as the sudden arrival, that alien being will vanish, and your former child of glory will peer out at you, as though they were just hiding behind a curtain for the last while ...

'It's hard to remember that you can keep loving them, in spite of not liking how they're behaving. Grab any opportunity of peace and conversation, without judgements and recriminations. Just enjoy the moments when the sun peeks out from behind the clouds.'

Tips from The Village on how to parent the alienation years

'Give them space, give them love and just remind them that you will always be there if they need to talk.' – **Lisa Joseph**

'I think my go to saying at that time to them was: "I still love you but I'm not loving this behaviour".' – **Michelle Cilliers**

'My approach is: "Stop being an ass and come cuddle your mom". So humour – a really good sense of humour – and not taking everything so seriously, works for us. Laugh at yourselves/them, alot.' – **Roxanne Van Der Schyff**

To which **Andréa Lubbe** responded: 'I love this, and in hindsight … my approach should have been: "Stop being an ass and go cuddle your son" 😉.'

Be consistent, suspend judgement and say sorry

'Although I think that I got the kids I did to learn all the life lessons I needed to learn, this surly stage drained my last drop of patience sometimes. It did give me three valuable lessons though:

1. **Be consistent.** While teens are going through this awful, hormonal, emotional and cognitive growth phase, their minds and bodies are chaotic places. They are often at odds with themselves – never mind everyone else. If you can be their rock, the one constant in their life that they can rely on to be there no matter how angry or distant or annoying or frustrating they are, you will be rewarded when the phase passes and you can still be the person your teen turns to.
2. **Learn to suspend your judgement.** Yes, there are times when it is necessary to be reactive before you can be proactive BUT if you want to be the person your teen turns to in tough times, they need to know that although you might be angry with them, you will 100% be there for them in a way that provides solutions and not judgement.
3. **Learn to apologise.** This was the toughest thing for me to learn how to do (because I'm always right 😉). Sometimes, even when you are in the right (or right), you need to model forgiveness. Whether you apologise for your tone, your bad mood, your not giving them a chance to speak, your knee-jerk reaction because you were worried or even an "I'm sorry I upset you",

by acknowledging that you recognise your own behaviour, you have reflected on the moment, and that an apology does not make you weak, in fact it makes you brave – apologising is a difficult thing to do, no matter how old you are.' – **Lesley Scott**, admin

Meet them where they are …

'I started watching F1 with my son and my hubby started playing games like Minecraft with our daughter. It kept the connection open for us. So I suppose we met our children at their interests. We changed the rules of engagement and instead of expecting them to come to us, we went to them. Sometimes it is as simple as watching an episode of whatever trash they are watching on youtube/netflix/primevideo and just holding your tongue on how absolutely mind-blowingly awful it is.' – **Wendy Bowyer van Blerk**

… but know when they need some space

'For me it's been: take a giant leap away. Wait for them to come to you. Still have all the usual in the home, i.e. dinner together, expectations for chores. But give them space. My one has had a very dark time. From 2020 to now. There were times I really thought she wasn't going to make it. She has. And I am starting to see a beautiful soul emerging.' – **Anonymous**

'After being with his dad all weekend, he will come home and hide in his room. I start to feel like I'm neglecting him so I go in to just say "Hi" and I get a "Mom! I JUST want some alone time!!!!" Lol. It took me a while to come to peace with the fact that being his mom sometimes means I am invisible, sometimes he sees me. So I let him be when he needs his alone time, knowing that he will come bouncing out of his room eventually and interrupt me, mid-Instagram post by diving on my bed saying, "Mom, let's talk. Let's have some

bonding time", which generally means I now need to watch him do tricks on his skateboard or skimboard in my small bedroom. Like a hundred times. On repeat. And then in a flash, he's gone. At bedtime, not being allowed to kiss him goodnight, he throws a "See u Friday", which tells me all is perfect in his world. Sigh, the beautiful joys.'
– **Beverley Scott-Brown**

Never ever shame them

'Pick your battles very carefully. You've done the work and instilled the values; now trust the job you've done. We might not like them very much when they behave like aliens but you can be sure they're not liking themselves either. No one will judge them more than they're judging themselves so be the place of unconditional love. Never shame them, just love them harder. This too shall pass.' – **Debra Wucherpfennig**

And never let them go

'When my dearest teenage daughter was going through the horrible phase, I saw this meme, and it changed the way I viewed her blowups forever. It still was hurtful and horrible, but I remembered that she feels so safe with me, because she knows I will not let go of her. I will not let her treatment of me, in that moment, affect my love for her. She is safe. Afterwards, we could talk about it and clear the air. Until the next time. However, she is an adult now, and we have good conversations, making sure that anything that comes up, is dealt with in a good and adult way.' – **Tillie Smith**, behavioural coach

Know that you are not alone

'I have a 16-year-old and at times parenting her is super tough. I've started following "Whitney Fleming, Playdates on Fridays" on FB.

Her posts on her teens have been super useful and insightful and made me realise I'm not alone and my teen's behavior is very normal. She's helped me step back on many occasions and handle situations very differently, often with a deep breath to start. Have a follow – I think you will love her. Good luck, I know it's super challenging.'
– Tamara Maneveld Billimore

The art of listening

Connection is so important during the tween and teen years but in the busyness of life and the moodiness of teenagedom, it can be hard. Faced with the boundary-testing and sullenness that is so normal for teens, a busy parent may just default to 'Listen to me' commands and expectations. But the way we forge the connection that will keep them safe and keep the lines of communication open, actually, is by listening to them.

Catherine Donaldson, a wise and forthright Villager, adds this valuable insight: 'Maybe in hindsight I look at that stage differently now. The primary school years are not always easy. And as a parent I realised that I needed to work on myself and my demons in order to actually "live" the lessons I was trying to teach my children.

'We parent based on the parent we had, situations or experiences we had. So we either mimic our own parents' style or the pendulum swings in the completely opposite direction. So first I think self assessment and awareness are key.

'Work on your own deep-rooted stuff and once that's in progress it becomes easier to deal with the 'difficult' preteen/teen mood change. Presenting that perfect parent image to the Joneses and to your child makes the child subconsciously feel the need to be 'perfect' themselves. We have bad days. We cannot always give our best – just the best we can on each day. So why expect more from them?

'Listen to them. Speak honestly to them. If their mood is rude to you, calm down first. Sit with them. Ask why they feel like they do.

Tell them it's ok to have down days. Or to have days where being happy, then sad, then emotional and not knowing why is probably due to hormone changes and at the same time trouble with friends going through similar.

'Explain that being emotional or wanting solitary time in their bedroom is ok. Explain that it's not ok to take that out on family members. Also know that you are their safe space. So if they have to hold it together all day at school and then are able to be and feel their real selves at home with you, it is actually a compliment.

'Listen. Be present. I wasn't really present for years: Trying to survive an emotionally, stressful job, no choice but to 'put work first'. I'm forgiving myself for that now. It doesn't need to be hours – 15 minutes in the evening per child; listen to them. Think back to how you felt at their age. And there's no need for what you or the world may deem as perfection or success. You be real. And allow them the same.'

Masking: A cautionary tale from an anonymous Villager

'I am an involved mama to a beautiful 13-year-old girl who is in Grade 7, as well as a younger son.

'My daughter is involved in sport at school, and has an amazing group of supportive, loving friends. They are fun, sporty and kind. She is a clever sausage who works hard and is loved by 99% of her teachers. She is polite, responsible, mischievous and funny. She is well-mannered, intuitive and sassy. Her friends lovingly joke that she is a teacher's pet. Said in kindness but also true! You get the picture.

'I am a sensible mom, wise, intuitive, supportive. Often class mom purely because I don't do drama, just disseminate info to parents as requested. I am at all sports events as I have my own business. Dad is very involved. We have a stable, loving marriage. No fighting. Kids feel hugely loved by both of us. We don't have a lot of money so there are not many holidays but we have a happy life.

'Two months ago, my daughter had yet another run-in with a particular teacher who keeps picking on her. Tired of trying to help her work through this scenario I called on the beloved school counsellor to help us navigate this road who has a great rapport with my daughter after four years of on and off therapy.

'After the first meeting, she calls me … And here is the clanger … My moody teenager is depressed and highly anxious. She is even questioning the reason for life. While currently not serious, there is the start of suicide ideation. My "typically" moody, sometimes happy, sometimes snappy teenager is not okay. And I had no idea how bad it was.

'We put it down to teenager moodiness. Purely, simply "teenagerness". She really isn't that bad. She was just a little off … But she wasn't. She was falling apart inside and we had no idea!

'If I hadn't made that call to the counsellor, where would she be in two years?

'I am the mom who knows all this stuff. I am the mom who "sees" her kids. But I had no idea it was this bad. So we called in the big guns and got her on meds the next day, under the supervision of the correct health professionals. And she carried on with therapy.

'Last night I was out and my husband sent me a message … she is belly laughing with her brother on our bed. He is putting on a show and she is in her element. Our girl is back. With the help of meds and therapy … we didn't "wait to see". We acted immediately.

'What still blows my mind is that we didn't see it for what it is. She hid it so well. She masks well. I think that even she didn't know how she was feeling. She just pushed it all down.

'All I keep thinking is "This is how it starts" – those parents who say "We had no idea" really do have no idea. So if your gut is telling you something is off, please listen to it. This could have ended so differently in a few years time.

'Our journey is not over, this is merely the start of a new chapter.'

Chapter 3

COMPASSIONATE BOYS, FEISTY GIRLS

If there is one post guaranteed to get the hackles of the usually serene Village bristling, it's a post that starts off on the subject of older teenage boys behaving badly. Drunken behaviour, sexually inappropriate behaviour, entitled behaviour, thoughtless behaviour ... any post on this subject will guarantee a fiery and defensive response:

'But what about the girls?' post infuriated Boy Parents in response, detailing the many ways they have found girls to be complicit or 'as bad' as the boys. Girls mock and judge the boys cruelly, they report. They lead them on, bully them. They are cliquey, mean and untrustworthy.

'The boys,' Boy Parents report, 'in these woke times, are terrified to approach *any* girl lest they put a foot wrong and are reported and "cancelled".'

Queasy on Monday mornings, parents report on the stormy seas of the weekend. Posts pop up about teens being disloyal and disrespectful to each other. Parents write of shockingly bad behaviour and the lack of gratitude and respect displayed in their friends' parents' houses. On the worst mornings there are tales of serious contraventions – where stupidity, naivety and alcohol have sent teens and young adults sailing into waters they cannot navigate. Stories of hurt feelings, abandonment, imploded friend groups and friendships ... and worse: danger, sexual misconduct and violence are reported in heartsore detail.

If we parents didn't know it already, it's clearly a jungle out there. How do we ensure that our kids learn and uphold beautiful values that have endured over the years, and also are allowed to be their own, equally beautiful, empowered selves?

How do we stop them from being 'those kids'?

Few parents these days believe that old-fashioned restriction and repression are the answers. But in our search for effective parenting paths, we find ourselves fighting against the onslaught of social media: the bad lessons, the toxic dreams and, often worse, the role models that TikTok serves up to our kids.

We parent in the long shadow of our own childhood experience, hoping that we won't repeat our parents' mistakes. Those rules by which many of our parents brought us up ('Speak when you're spoken to,' 'Don't be cheeky,' 'Don't contradict me') do not resonate with us, or work on our children. And yet what a teen or young adult needs to thrive and succeed, in 2024 and beyond, is a hybrid of the good of the old and the brilliant of the *now*: how do we raise compassionate, polite, empathetic boys and strong, independent girls? How do we do this, while nurturing a confident and loving relationship?

Our cultures and our own upbringing can sometimes be unhelpful in trying to answer this question. With greater freedom and exposure, with progress, come complications, for sure.

Finding a new path and why it's so important

Vanessa says

The traditional roles (good girl/strong boy – aka timid, obedient girl/stoical, silent, repressed boy) can still cast a long shadow over our own parenting and our children's behaviour. Girls will be girls and boys will be boys remains the stew in which many of our families marinate.

Many years ago, I interviewed the legendary South African self-defence guru Sanette Smit. Describing South Africa's chilling gender-based violence statistics, she remarked that, in her many interviews with rapists and their victims, a trend emerged: the men felt inadequate and enraged; the women felt neither entitled nor empowered.

She described men of all races and socioeconomic groups who could not find employment and success; who could not provide for families; whose self-esteem had been destroyed by apartheid and its aftermath. She described boys who'd been mocked if they'd cried or showed vulnerability or tenderness when they were young; men who were encouraged to display aggression to gain respect as they aged. She described girls who'd been brought up (even in this day and age) to wait on the boys and elevate them, subtly or not, to a position of power they could not attain themselves.

'Who cooks?' she asked. 'Who serves? Who gets sent to university to be an engineer? Who washes up? Who is allowed to cry? Who is equipped to value themselves and also look after each other? The inevitable clash between men who aren't compassionate and girls who don't believe they are "powerful" or "independent" remains a dangerous and toxic combination,' she said.

I recently posted this question on The Village (referring to the kind of values that have endured over the years, and not the kind of old-fashioned thinking we've left behind as it no longer serves society): 'How do we teach our children beautiful old-fashioned values – respect (for their elders, employers, peers and parents), good manners, hard work, helping out – while at the same time still ensuring that they are feisty, courageous, self-confident and bold?' One effective tool is to upend the traditional: to emphasise unconventional boy and girl roles for our *children. As Sanette's research has shown, the need for this is deeper than merely a parental desire for well-behaved teenage guests on any given weekend.*

Here are some of the answers I received.

As usual, it starts with us ...

'How do we teach our children old-fashioned values while ensuring that they are feisty, courageous, self-confident and bold? By modelling those values,' said **Judy MacGregor** – and by being 'compassionate dads and fearless feisty moms', added **Laura Lagertha**.

'Children learn from what they see too. So if people in a home treat one another with respect, this becomes ingrained,' wrote **Jane Dawson**. 'When they are rude to someone this needs to be addressed. I have three adult children and two teenage granddaughters and manners and respect are inherent.'

'It's holding that rope when they try to pull you over. It's showing them you value yourself in micro moments so that they are left in no doubt as to what you'd accept even from them,' said **Amanda Stergianos**. 'It's being a parent and not a buddy. It's being innately kind every single day. Most importantly, it's connection over correction.'

Susan van Aardt says we set the standard. 'Lead by example. Allow your children to see you stand up for yourself and to see you prioritise self-care, good work ethic, setting boundaries and being a good friend to others.'

'Let them see you break. Show them real emotions and talk about them. Address shitty behaviour immediately and explain to them that you love them very much but not so much what they did,' advised **Sam Brown**. 'Show them your worth from the get-go and BELIEVE IT YOURSELF!' she continued. 'Oh, and don't swear in front of the little sods when they first learn to speak or they will tell everyone you ever meet that Mommy/Daddy said a bad and that word was ...! Mostly they'll do this in public.'

'Model kindness to your sons,' wrote **Jill Schulman**. 'Expect it back from them. Teach them from a young age to speak about their feelings – allow big feelings, identify and name them. Learn to search for who your son is so that you can draw out the best parts of him and strengthen the weaker parts. Advocate for him and let him see that you are in his corner ... but also expect him to speak up for others. Allow him to be the best version of himself, rather than the best version you might want him to be. Look – hard – for the very best things about him and allow him to hear you speak often of your admiration of those qualities. Love him fiercely and let him know it. Expect him to love back and teach him ways to show it. Be the best version of yourself you can find in yourself to be ... and allow him to see you trying, every day, to rise above.

'For your daughters: all the above, accept her ... And let her see your strength. Expect strength back from her – groom her to use her voice. And allow her to use it – wisely – on you.'

... And it starts early

'Time, love and boundaries in the early years as so much of empathy and the important human qualities are forged in the first five years,' wrote **Sarah Bailey**. 'As a therapist I see the impact when the first years are not optimal.'

Tanya Kahn Daniel said, 'Children learn through modelled behaviour. Be the change you wish to see in the world. Show kindness and compassion to others and explain to your children why you behave in that manner. Smile at strangers, compliment random people, thank the teller/packer/waitron/security guard. No person forgets kindness, so be the difference and live a life where you are unforgettable.'

'You have to set a good example! You have to start with the basics when they're very young. You can't wait until they're older, then think a magic solution will materialise. There have to be boundaries from the word "Go" and reminders about "Please and thank you" until it becomes a habit. It was always the last thing my Mum would say when I was off to a party: "Remember your pleases and thank yous" ... I did the same with my children and they in turn have done the same with their children. Good manners are hugely important,' said **Elaine McLaren**.

'I think all of it stems from the concept of respect. If you treat other people with respect, you demonstrate manners, you help other people; and if you treat *yourself* with respect, you can model "both" and so your child sees you being polite, feisty AND courageous,' said **Nicki Minchin**.

'So how do you teach your children respect?' she continued. 'You treat them with respect. From the cradle. Shouting at them is not showing respect, hitting them is not showing respect, being discourteous to them is not showing them respect.

'Listening to them, giving them a place at the table is showing respect. And as importantly, is showing them you respect yourself. If they shout at you or use bad manners, you emphasise how they are disrespecting you. You show them respect, you treat teachers, employees, waiters, shop staff, other children with respect.

'You explain to them how your own self-respect has guided you. You cannot teach your children respect for other people or themselves unless you, as parents, demonstrate it. It doesn't happen all the time. Sometimes we mess up. And this is a good time to raise this subject with them. It's not an easy fix. But one that is our responsibility.'

'Teach children to set boundaries and know their worth!' said **Natasha Reeler**. 'I also tell my son that every girl/woman is someone's daughter or sister. He must treat them how he would want someone to treat his younger sister.'

Wash, rinse, repeat

'Manners are taught – repetition, repetition and repetition,' wrote **Lisa Hansen**. 'They can be courageous, feisty *and* be taught manners?

My motto from young was manners maketh a man. Reminders are still given daily, so hoping it's sunk in most of the time!'

'Manners and respect should be part of our core values,' said **Annette Kruger**. 'By making it part of your life it should eventually come naturally to our children.'

Help them find their voices

Peter-Francy Schoeman said, 'I only have a daughter, so can't actually comment on boys. Teach your daughters about consequences. Allow them to make mistakes. So they learn that even when they make mistakes you love them and forgive them but they will have to face the consequences of their actions. The one thing they must be secure of, above all, is that your love is unconditional. You are there to comfort them, but can't fix every problem.

'Encourage individual thinking and always be available to LISTEN but let them find their own solutions. Value their ideas. Let them know their opinion counts.

'Tell them they can achieve anything they put their mind to. Teach them that it's okay to fail. Pick yourself up and try again. It's better to fail, than to have never tried.'

'Allow them their voices. I find my son to be a naturally compassionate human. I think it has to do with the challenges he has faced with his sister's health from day dot. He rises every day to being beyond my wildest imagination as a compassionate person,' said one Village member. 'My daughter has always been allowed to say her say. She is not a shrinking violet and knows her voice should be heard. We have had to teach her to use her voice kindly and with consideration. Using your voice does not need to be hurtful.'

'Talk openly about anything and everything, not only certain subjects with one, certain subjects with the other: Bodies, politics, language, school, dating, relationships, friendships, ideals and ideas, how the world works, different cultures, travel, money, etc. Be curious about their opinions and listen, listen, listen!' wrote **Suna Hall**.

'I have a fearless, feisty daughter. Don't know what I did right but me and her dad's face would always light up when we see her and listen to her stories and ideas from when she was small and still at 25,' said **Suzanne Wiese**. 'I once read that that is what kids need – to really be seen and heard.'

Carmen Andries's daughter had to have a difficult conversation with family members so Carmen suggested some role play first to go over what she would be saying and how she planned to say it. 'So that I could guide and correct the behaviour and the body language. I think practising at home, and parents also mirroring kind behaviour, helps a lot. They learn from what they hear and see.'

Love them hard

'Unconditional love!!! Yes, boundaries and consequences are important but they need to know that you love them no matter what and that you have their back!' suggested **Charnelle Munitich**. 'Encouraging them to be fearless and follow their dreams no matter how scary it may be in that very moment as that moment is just that, a moment but the outcome will last a lifetime.'

'Don't laugh: My boys have always had a dog. Caring for and loving a pet teaches empathy and compassion in the best way possible. I believe a family fur baby is the greatest gift of love,' said **Pam Goldacre**.

Same but different?

'I can tell you how my parents raised me to be feisty; they raised me to be a man. There was no such thing as boys do this and girls do that. It was always "If a boy can do it, so can you". Extended family made comments such as "Marry a rich man" but my dad said, "If you want to be successful one day you need to [insert advice of the day]" and it was never limited to what girls do or don't do,' **Roelien Kruger** remembers.

'My parents moved heaven and earth,' she continued, 'to help me get back into maths (I dropped it in Grade 10), so that I could do higher grade Computer Science as I was slaying all the boys in programming. There was no such thing as "Girls don't code" from them or my teacher. What that meant was that the language spoken to me was the same as that spoken to the boys. I wasn't dumbed down when I told them my dream of being an attorney or accountant. I was simply told what I needed to do to get there.

'I got the opposite from some teachers. Sad, but true. "Attorney? Why not become a paralegal instead?" "Accountant? Why not become a bookkeeper or office manager?" Because it wasn't my career path. Not my dream. I haven't worked my butt off to be an admin manager! (No offence to anyone who is, it's a very important job – not for me though). My job wasn't even admin-based. I was a consultant.

'Think of this example. Does it sound familiar? Three kids: the sons got university educations but the daughter got sent off to a college to study travel and tourism. That thinking, right there, is key to shaping stereotypes of boys and girls.

'So don't push kids to follow careers usually earmarked for a certain gender. If your son says he wants to be a nurse, be happy and ask him what his plans are to get there. Don't correct him and say he should rather be a doctor. If your daughter says she wants to be a high court judge, don't correct her and tell her to rather be a paralegal.

'Our language and how we speak to our children matters! There should be no gender specific language in our speech except for biological related situations like period or puberty etc. But jobs, life, relationships? NO.'

As **Annelise Drewes Giddings** encouraged us, 'Applaud and encourage character and growth in terms of kind, brave, strong, caring, helpful etc. instead of telling little girls they are just cute or beautiful and little boys that they are tough.' And, 'Treat your boys AND girls with tenderness, give them heaps of affection,' offered **Claire Murning Oosthuizen**. 'Allow them to feel their own emotions without criticism. Share your own moments of insecurity, weakness, regrets and your mistakes. Apologise when you were wrong, out of line or too depleted to do the right thing. Discuss situations that arise, try to consider what you/they see as the other person's point of view and try to remind them of when they felt similar feelings. Commend your girls whenever they speak up for themselves or others. Tell them to never stop speaking their truth.'

'Don't ever say the likes of "Cowboys don't cry" to boys. Let them cry,' advised **Kathryn Molyneaux**. 'If they're hurt, let them cry; if they're sad, let them cry; hey, if they're happy, let them cry! Talk openly about feelings, their own feelings and how they make others feel. And the best thing you can ever be, above all else, is kind.' **Jo Facey Pentz** echoed this sentiment: 'Show compassion in all you do, especially in respect of the fact that boys and men are sensitive beings. And be feisty, fun and fabulously unintimidated!'

Natalie Glitterflip recommended the following: 'For daughters, teach them to speak for themselves as soon as they are able to form a coherent sentence. At restaurants, teach her to order her meal. At the deli, let her order her sandwich. Everywhere, teach her how to address the adult with respect and state her needs. When they are that little they aren't shy, but they are overlooked by adults. When we teach them how to speak up, place an order, we are teaching them to verbalise their needs outside of the home. I am so glad that I did this with my daughter; she is 12 and confident to speak for herself, voice her needs without feeling embarrassed, a skill I only partially mastered by the time I was 22.' And **Darryl Lampert** gave this advice: 'Teach your daughters to invest and save from an early age so that they never get stuck in a job or relationship where they have to stay due to a lack of their own money.'

'Encourage them to do as much for themselves as possible from as young as possible,' said **Kirsty Galliard**. 'Empower them with life skills like tidying up after themselves, doing chores, and being responsible and accountable to manage their own homework/projects/school schedules, activities and extra-murals. Obviously, with our support and assistance where required. This builds a good work ethic, the ability to manage their time and plan ahead and helps them remember to be considerate of others as they learn to give us proper notice when they need project supplies or lifts.'

Heidi Maggott had a word of warning: 'Keep calm and don't lose the plot when the girls turn their feisty fearlessness back on you; it comes as a shock.'

Respect is earned – and it goes both ways

While **Mandy Duff Aucamp** said, 'It's not easy to find balance with teens, but when it comes to the important stuff like manners and treating people (regardless of who they are) with respect? I am non-negotiable', **Andrew Collins** felt that, 'You, as parent, must earn your child's respect and your child must earn your respect'.

Gavin Fish expanded on this theme: 'When I started teaching, unquestioning respect for an adult was a given, simply because you were an adult; later on it became "I will respect you if you live what you teach, are genuine, authentic"; more recently, "I will respect you if I like you and agree with you". The point is not that we should therefore become likeable and agreeable, but that we should be true to our word and model what we say. Teens see through adult inconsistency in an instance (and particularly ADHD teens, but that's for a different day).'

'Raise them to treasure and respect someone else's heart,' added **Nicolee Bowers**.

Wise words

Debbie Owen noted that, 'When it comes to compassion, the advice people often comment on is my reminder to "lift others as you rise". Whenever I'm asked, I tell youngsters that their job is to grab the opportunities provided to them and to use them to rise ... and when they rise, to always look around at those who might be struggling to do the same, and to lift them. Oh yes – and just be lekker.'

'Don't let the compliments of others build you up otherwise their criticism will break you down. Be secure and confident in your own identity,' said **Liza Lindeque**.

'I think it also takes a village,' wrote **Liezel Gruhn Topat**. 'As a mom, an aunt to many now-adult nieces and nephews, and friends, I treat them all as my own, and manners and respect are very high on my list. Children/teens often respond well to other adults and are better behaved when out of parental reach. So teach them all, whoever they belong to.'

Chapter 4
SHOUTING ACROSS THE ABYSS

Somewhere between 6 and 13, we get some previews of the sass and resistance we can expect in the teens. The sweetness of early childhood begins to wear off.

After 13, between the mostly sass and resistance, we only sometimes catch glimpses of the sweetness we remember.

Having children is a slow process of letting go. Sometimes the distancing happens at a good pace everyone can cope with, and sometimes it is too fast for us, or them, to handle well. There are these sudden gaping holes between members of the family. We've been preoccupied with sick parents, or they've been busy with school or sport. They've lost themselves in gaming or in activism or in those epic sleeps teenagers sometimes seem to require.

We've lost ourselves in coping.

We've been zoned out, or they have been.

Or there's been fighting and shouting and crying and right now we're all just a little bit sick of one another.

These abysses between us and them yawn from time to time and when we suddenly see them, we can be hit by an almighty nostalgia for the easy times when playing came naturally and talking was easy.

Tanya Kahn Daniel shared this on The Village group: 'For me, the most important thing is finding ways to ensure our connection to our children remains strong and grows with them. As much as we want our kids to remain little (and us to remain in control), it's so vital to have shared learning experiences. Take them on adventures, let them take you on adventures. Grow together. Step out of your comfort zones together and do different things. Live, not exist.'

Vanessa says

An eminent psychologist with a specialisation in young adults says there's something about communicating with adolescents and young adults in a way that is not face to face that is hugely helpful. She said that so many kids she had seen at her practice in Gauteng said their happiest family memories were of Kruger Park holidays, with everyone in the car chatting, singing, looking for animals.

Another friend says that hiking – for young men, particularly – works because they are not eye to eye with, or under the glare of, their parents or other adults who are trying to engage them. Some young men find it much easier to talk in this way.

Take the parental pressure and scrutiny away! If your child can see past you and your concern or pressure, they may be better able to describe what they are seeing. And what worries them or interests them about it.

Melanie Jenkins wrote, 'We have just got back from a 3 000-km road trip from the Kgalagadi with our 2 ... they are young adults, not teens, but it was fabulous for all of us. No TV, no signal, just animal spotting, lots of silly jokes and awesome fun'.

Julie Hall said: 'We did a road trip through the Karoo during the holidays. It was such a nice reset. Trivia games, music playlists and ham-and-cheese sarmies. The best!'

This from **Saul Smith**: 'Best time to connect – however long or short – are those times in the car … loads of sharing goes on here … for us at least.'

And from **Moira Honman Coady**: 'Before he left home (at 27 …) I used to offer to collect my son from work even if it was 10pm or actually especially if it was 10 at night. The drive home meant he appreciated me coming out that late and he couldn't escape a chat. I would not ask hard questions or complain or anything negative but plan positive remarks and conversations (tell him funny things about work). A bit of silence too. Not all trips were as chatty as I would have liked but it definitely strengthened the bond which was 'breaking' due to other pressures we both had. 2 years later, he's a Dad, lives in another country but WhatsApps every night and says "I love you" before I do instead of grudgingly afterwards. When I think of my boy and his little family, my heart bursts with joy.'

Other kinds of side by side

Petrol is expensive and there are other ways to be side by side: walks, runs, washing and drying the dishes by hand, painting a wall, washing a dog, making a big deal about watching a favourite series together again because of how much you laughed together last time. Villagers had these suggestions:

'Watch some comedy and laugh our heads off. Our boys are 15 and 16 – we watch everything from Marc Lottering to Kevin Hart. Trevor Noah is usually a hit.' – **Neesa Moodley**

'He shares my passion and patience at game reserves. We can sit at a watering hole for hours. We love going to see theatre productions and museums too.' – **Julie Hall**

'Cooking together (assuming there's some level of interest and enjoyment). You are working in parallel, focused on a task and chatting, rather than eyeball-to-eyeball Having A Talk.' – **Kate Sidley**

'We create an Oscars Watch list during school holidays. To be fair there are only the 2 of us, so it's quite simple. One of us picks a movie – our choice of genre and decade – and we sit together and watch, and then rate it. The movie list starts waaaay before holidays, written in a small book. After the movie we rate it – mark down scores. Tally it up. (Just saying my choice of movies from the 80s have won 3 years in a row 😁 but it's not a competition!!)' – **Lauren Reynders**

Play that again

We get so serious when life gets tough and without even knowing it, a whole family – whether of two people or five with some grandfolks and pets thrown in – can get really miserable and cope-y, just getting through. We forget that humans like to play – even adult humans. Playfulness is an attitude (and some people are more naturally playful than others), but that attitude can dampened by life-with-a-capital-L.

We can't really do rough and tumble with teens any more, but doing sporty things can be a shortcut to physical play: ping-pong, beach bats, Swingball, badminton, boules and French cricket are games anyone can play pretty much anywhere (okay, not the ping-pong if you don't have a table).

Ten-pin bowling, ice-skating and putt-putt are pretty standard and reasonably accessible family-outing possibilities. Hikes and family walks are good for everyone.

Hopscotch and jump rope don't get old, even if we do.

Then there are inside games. We asked Villagers for their favourites:

Most often mentioned Village favourites

- Catan
- Scrabble
- Bananagrams
- Uno
- Uno Flip!

Other mentions

Monopoly is still a huge favourite after all these years but, if you play it, you might want to heed Villager **Jonathan Hoffenberg**'s warning: 'Just stay away from Monopoly. It's an evil, divisive game that has a history of a real male douchebag stealing a great idea from a decent Scottish woman who just wanted to educate the poor on the dangers of landlords.'

Don't forget about Monopoly Deal, Cluedo, 30 Seconds, Pictionary, Balderdash, Magic: The Gathering, poker, rummy, 21, Crazy Eights and Canasta.

Sarah Oosthuizen came up with this suggestion: 'Call me morbid, but I've actually asked myself this question: If I knew that I only had months left on this earth, what would I do? My answer had nothing to do with seeing far-flung places, or doing daring deeds. I decide that I'd read aloud to my children.

'It's fitting, really, because it will close the loop on birth-to-death. I read Narnia's Prince Caspian aloud (in puffs and pants) gyrating on my birthing-ball, to poor wide-eyed father-to-be, hours before welcoming our first born. And then it turned to good-night stories. And then read-alouds to all the children, as we huddled and cuddled together over books that flung us across worlds and ages. They'd sit around me sketching, building LEGO, creating worlds without and within. We traveled together.

'And so, when the itchy-scratchiness of growing up and away happens, or when we are just tired by life's demands, it's to the couch and bed we retreat. Together – with me reading, accents trying, discussions flying. Hearts become impassioned – together. Or restful – still together.

'This is our refuge when we need to come together. Other worlds, social issues, compassion and passion bind us through a medium that is both separate, but together.'

Use a combo and always be open to the moments of connection that present themselves

Lauren Clack said, 'I've struggled with [connecting across the abyss], just feeling like I didn't have the answers at the time (and still don't). But the attempt at 'kinship' took various different forms over the years – from getting MacDonalds and going to park somewhere with a great view and just chatting, to weekends away just the two of us, to movies, or long car drives when convo just felt easier than at home. Watching godawful TV series she was into also went a long way (and sometimes they weren't ALL bad, like discovering Henry Cavill in The Witcher!)

'I did find though, that often the nice moments of connection came unforced, at random times, and when I wasn't trying so hard.'

And as Zama Pienaar mentioned, 'I learnt to utilise technology to my advantage, but also be mindful of its impact on relationships. We connect through text messages, video calls, or social media, but balance it with face-to-face interactions. I'm not talking about them being outside the house, but even in the house at times, not always.

'I'm also the type of parent that apologises when I'm wrong and in turn they learnt to do the same.

'I celebrate their achievements no matter how small.

'I also check their schedule so that we can go on dates. Our dates are not just to restaurants but even to the botanical gardens and Klapperkop Nature reserve. It's free but allows the mind to rest and brings tranquility.'

'I have 3 gorgeous guys', said **Tanya Kahn Daniel**, 'and what I do is make a point of going on a date with them individually. It can be anything from a quick coffee to a long walk. Also try to find interesting things we are both keen to investigate and we do them together. As a family, now that our boys are older teens – I have started adventure Sundays. We find something, somewhere we want to explore or try out and off we go! Some are great and some can be disastrous but we have fun, we laugh and most importantly we make memories.'

Take a break from one another

This anonymous parent and her daughter needed space. Here's what she did:

'I had got to the stage where I hated who I was becoming as a parent as much as the situation we were experiencing with my daughter because of how I was reacting and responding and I ended up doing something I never thought I would do.

'I asked my ex to take her for two weeks and I realized during the time that I did this for more reasons that I thought. It was the first time he has spent two weeks with her since she was 1.5 years old and for once he was 100% fully supportive of the entire situation. He saw in two weeks why and how we felt the way we did. I saw it as an intervention for us BOTH. I needed the time out just as much as to have a hard look at myself, my contribution to the situation and to determine which trajectory I wanted our relationship to take and what I needed to do.

'I realized a lot of things and also what I had enabled to happen by allowing the path of disrespect to happen towards me, our family and our home to continue to such a point in the name of empathy towards all she had gone through. Because there has been a lot of huge disappointments and enormous health challenges stopping her sporting career and well, just such a lot, I went into sympathy mode but I also went too far.

'She has been home for nearly two weeks and there has been a shift between us made possible because both of us want to heal and reconnect ... I understand part of why we were constantly bashing heads and being destructive, being resentful and not "hearing" each other.'

When reconnecting becomes impossible, just sit it out

Anthea Katzeff had this story to share on The Village: 'Dear fellow parental units. I've noticed many questions on the group regarding the struggles of raising teens and the conundrum of having young adults and the looming of the empty nest syndrome.

'I'd like to reassure you all that generally, if you've done your job right, it's all going to be ok. I can't speak for every family or situation but at the end of it all, it's going to be ok. They will be fine, you'll find yourself again and the world should even out for you.

'Not long ago I had twin daughters who couldn't speak to each other or connect with us, girls who had to live the best years of their lives in lockdown and somehow pass matric at the end of it all with psyches in tact and a family unit that still functioned. To add, a Bull in a china shop pubescent boy child with [Asperger's] who took great glee in pushing the buttons of every member of the family and terrorising his sisters to the point that they were afraid of him. And ... a husband working from the room upstairs. One twin ended up with an eating disorder and the other with PTSD from having to carry the secrets of her sister for so long. I had not a hope in hell nor a lifeline other than this group, which I was too proud to tap into and where I sought solace in the fact that there were other families out there as f&cked up as mine.

'I remember feeling spent at the end of every day having to be the grounding for my 3 children and the bonus child (husband). There were arguments, demands (mostly irrational), shouting matches and much hiding from each other In the only free room of the house being the bar, which we would fight over as to who would get to go down there at any given moment in time. There was no solace, no reprieve and no end in sight. Quite frankly, most of the time I felt that I had failed as a parent, a partner and a human being.

'My daughters grew up, passed matric, split up for the first time in their lives and became incredible adults independently. In fact more incredible than I could ever have hoped for. My son is an almost 16 year old gentle giant with more empathy in his little finger than any of the men I knew growing up. These children that I held no hope for at one point, suddenly became logical thinking, intelligent, emotionally aware and powerful young adults (and teen).

'We made mistakes along the way, we sometimes, as parents, weren't the people we should have been, to each other and to our children but in general we did the right thing, instilled good values, taught our children all the things that were lacking in the previous generation for various reasons. Hit miss, hit miss. Always there was love. Even when we were furious or disappointed our children knew that they were loved. When they leave us and they're confident and joyful, it means we've succeeded and our heartache is ours alone to bear because we were merely their custodians all along. And that is our [cue] to go out and be joyful and youthful once again.

'There is no magic recipe. There is no formula for raising good humans because every child and parent is different, every situation unique. What makes us human is the ability to adapt to any situation and hopefully make the right choices (mostly) and when we don't we get up and try again!

'Please, all of you who are struggling, it will all be ok as long as the decisions you make come from a place of love and not ego. Believe it or not, love does indeed have the power to conquer all. Not always but mostly.

'I wish you all luck and a deep well of love to dip into to enable you to raise the best kind of humans possible. From my heart to yours ...'

Chapter 5
'MY HOUSE, MY RULES'

One of the most easily dispensed and often-used advice from Villagers to other Villagers are the words 'My house, my rules'. Let's take a deeper dive on this one.

Melanie Loebenberg-Novitzkas had this to say on the group: 'The one thing I read too often (on The Village) is a 'My House, My Rules' statement, and it always bothers me. Why does this statement rankle for some parents, while others use it almost as the rallying cry whenever their authority is challenged even in the slightest?

'There is always at least one kid in the house that will go and on and on with the "Whys" and the "It's-so-unfairs" when a line has been drawn. In cases like that, saying "My house, my rules" can be the final nail in the coffin of the argument if you decide to disengage from the discussion then.

'But using it as a first resort can lessen its impact when you really need this big gun. It does come across as authoritarian, inflexible and old-fashioned – in a bad way.'

And **Yvonne Brogan** wrote: 'I grew up in the My rules, My way generation, with no voice. I may have given my daughter too much voice in compensation; I won't change that though. Kids have thoughts and feeling too. Talk to them, learn from them.'

To which another Villager responded: 'Agree with this 99.999% (actually 100% but I need to maintain a 0.001% justification for my own sanity when I eventually do shut my nagging ADHD 6-year-old down for asking me "Why" after 3728191916284956 explanations 😊). But in more seriousness, it should never be about the notion of 'rules' anyway, it should be an ongoing and open discussion about strategies and family agreements. Those times when a parent really does need to draw a line as the responsible person, it should be a boundary instead of a rule, and even if the child can't fundamentally understand or agree with the boundary you can explain and contextualise the concept of boundaries and your role as a parent.'

The rules

Part of the confusion has to do with the word itself. Here are the first and second definitions of the word 'rule' according to the Oxford Dictionary:

1. One of a set of explicit or understood regulations or principles governing conduct or procedure within a particular area of activity;
2. The control of or dominion over an area or people.

The first meaning implies agreement and accommodation. Heaving out 'My house, my rules' at every sticking point has much more of a control-and-dominion mood.

In response to Melanie's post, **Michelle Shorkend Koton** wrote, 'Also dislike that blanket statement so much. Just feels so like a dictatorship and the taking advantage of power.'

As Melanie said, 'The house is the home of all who live there. The kids, the dogs, the 'rents. Choose your rules and your hard no's and what you are prepared to compromise on. Some rules are negotiable and some are simply not. Respect goes both ways and so does apologising when you messed up. We want well-rounded, balanced individuals who are critical thinkers and respect themselves and others and creating the environment for them to become good humans starts when they are little. Mine are now 18, 20 and 26, and we had some hairy times, but there was always autonomy and mutual respect in our mostly peaceful home.'

How many people are in 'your' house?

The reason **Caryn Pottas** said she didn't like the phrase 'My house, my rules' was because 'You don't want your kids thinking that they don't actually belong in the home'.

No one is arguing that you pay the rent or the bond, work your fingers to the bone, and generally sacrifice way more than anyone is ever going to notice, but you don't live alone. Rules are precisely *not* for one person. They usually emerge in any shared spaces – like homes and schools – and exist for good reasons: safety, community, fairness, consideration and respect. Everyone is expected to follow them for the smooth running of life where people are together.

'I think we can differentiate between "My house, my rules" and "Our home, our rules",' **Lesmarie Williams** says. 'The hard no's are "My house rules" (no drugs, no stealing, when younger no room hopping, no smoking in the house the non-negotiables) respect to the house owners who do fund the house. The lesser no's can be debated as home rules. These has to be a distinction between the 2 I think. And yes mutual respect is important!'

It's true, families aren't really democracies. Adults have to adult, otherwise the young would be brought up by the young and that's never been a great idea. Plus, rules make children feel safe and contained and eliminate confusion.

Rules that have become outdated, or were bad, nonsensical or discriminatory to start with, can and should be changed.

The single most useful thing to know about rules, as a parent, is that if they are understood and agreed on by the family, compliance is easier for everyone. As **Alison Roberts Theron** wrote: 'Why we do things as we do in our family. Mutual respect, boundaries that are agreed upon and understood. That sort of thing. Teens who are part of the decision-making process. Less bossiness and more collaboration and community.'

Teens, rules and boundaries

It is mostly understood that part of the job of being a teenager is to test the boundaries to make sure they're solid, to challenge rules, and generally to make a nuisance of yourself to parents who suddenly have to think a bit a harder about why they hold a certain position.

This is the way in which the world keeps itself young and discourages rigid thinking.

When your children question your rules, it usually means it's time for a re-evaluation.

Kerry Donaldson offered this nugget: 'I reckon if you cannot provide a logical and coherent argument for any single rule, then you shouldn't be enforcing it.'

Debby Shackleton-Pretorius said that for five years she drove her son and four other boys home most afternoons. Their school was 20 kilometres across town through roadworks and heavy traffic and so discussions could last between half an hour and an hour. Here is her story:

'The other boys were often amazed by my openness to debate, and my willingness to change my mind or my answer if they could show me that I had been narrow-minded or that I didn't have all the facts.

'My husband and I were always open to our teenage son's opinions and viewpoints but there were certainly many times when my no remained no. While it often wasn't happily accepted, they honoured my decision.

'Quite often our debate opened the scope of our discussions to include other issues that I hadn't been aware of. In my opinion, our relationship was closer because we took the time to really understand each other's points of view.

'They are still welcome to challenge my opinions and offer their views and I can assure you that I continue to learn from them. And they still learn from me. It's a win-win situation, because we developed respect for each other at an early age.'

Catherine Hermans wrote: 'I am known as "The Cool Mom". Now. ☺ 😉 My eldest and I chatted about it recently. Yes I was the strict one. But with each "No" there was a "Why". As single moms the decision making is always a tough one. Now they both are out of the house and I know the "No's" paid off. Even with my students, they knew … follow my few house rules and you will have the best housemom ever! ☺ ☺'

When someone in The Village was complaining about how her daughter wouldn't do as she was told, **Hedwig Claire Scheepers** wrote: 'Time to sit down and listen to your daughter. You give a long list of instructions that you expect your daughter to follow. Which is helpful, but what are her own desires, requirements and wishes? What rules and boundaries do you have to respect in a home that you share? Raising balanced adults doesn't happen via a list of instructions that our teens must follow. We need to model respect. We need to be able to hear a point of view we do not agree with and find the merit, or help our kids discover, without judgment, why there is no merit …'

Do rules exist to be broken?

A discussion on The Village about hair rules at school was a great example not only of the pros and cons of rules, but of how to have constructive conversations in which parties agree and disagree on various points, without bludgeoning one another. In fact, it's the kind of discussion that makes for great dinner-table conversation about what rules are for. Here it is:

'Hair is political, not logical. Short hair for boys is possibly an intersection of military (uniform, discipline, follow orders, conform), industrial (clock-driven, age and subject separated, rows of desks, standardised curriculum and assessment), patriarchy (clear line between "boy" and "girl"), colonial (does "neat" hair start with an Anglo-Saxon baseline?), class (affording wigs, weaves, colours), identity (signalling group membership, or anti-group hippies or skin-heads).

'It isn't just hair and nothing else. So, now the answer to your question is the answer to your politics and your child's politics: do you want one rule for all implemented at the country level, or allow multiple different rules at each community/school level, or fewer rules? There are pros and cons to each ... and isn't this a "fairly safe" and fun topic for our kids to flex their critical thinking muscles and learn about all these illogical boundaries we have, and then choose: love it, accept it, change it, or leave it?' – **Roy Hobson**

His post elicited a huge response and **Ron McGregor** had this to say:

'Wow, so many replies, and plenty of valid insights, too.

'It's a rather philosophical question this. Does long hair impact on the ability to learn? Absolutely not. Then why do it? Those who believe in such rules, AND have thought about them, might answer that school and growing up are not just about learning academic subjects. They are also about learning how to fit into society. Whether we like it or not, if we survive to age 21, we are going to have to live in this thing called society. And society, by its very nature, accepts very few rebels or loners. If you want a job, you need to fit in with the company. If you want to start a company, you need to be accepted by the people you are going to employ. If you want to have a social life, you will need to be accepted by your friends and family. So, the process of school, along with the process of growing up, includes learning about which rules you should comply with, and which rules you may make for yourself. Schools make rules. Some of them are sound rules, and some of them are silly – or, at least, they are silly to some, but not to others.

But the whole point is that they are rules. If you want to go to School X, you agree to abide by the rules of School X. If you prefer the rules of School Y, then you go to School Y. You cannot demand that School X must change its rules to suit you. All society is built on a foundation of social compliance. People abide by the rules if they want to fit in. Within society as a whole are many mini-societies. If you want to play in a symphony orchestra, you abide by the rules of the conductor. If you don't like them, you look for another orchestra. If you want to play a game of rugby, you abide by the rules of the game as interpreted by the referee. You can't tell the ref, or the rugby administrators, that the rules pertaining to the line-out are a lot of rubbish and must be changed because you, personally, disagree with them. If you don't like the rules of rugby, maybe you should try hockey, ping-pong, or darts. But they have rules, too.

'There's also a clear understanding that, when you cease membership of something, then you are freed from the rules of that something. So, if you want to attend a particular school, you have to accept that attendance requires acceptance of the rules. But you won't be at that school forever. When you finish you will no longer be subject to those rules. Of course, if a rule is patently ridiculous, and a lot of people feel that way, it is always possible to make representation to have the rule changed. But one does not start disobeying the rule before it has been changed. That's anarchy. The civilised procedure would be to get the rule changed, and then everyone is freed from its constraints. When I was at school, ages ago, I also had problems with the rules about wearing my hair like the Beatles. It was a fight I was never going to win. It was a very fine school, and my parents were never going to let me give it up for a lesser school just so that I could have longer hair. Once I left school, I grew my hair to shoulder length. Not being able to have long hair at school did me no harm at all. (My general madness is attributable to all manner of other causes!)

That school also had a whole lot of other rules which I thought pretty damned silly, but I obeyed them. It taught me that society is stronger when people agree to abide by rules and operate together.

My hair is pretty long right now. But I left school a long time ago, so I'm entitled!'

He added later that rules could be questioned and challenged when they didn't make sense. '[I] believe it is essential that there are people who continue to challenge unfair, unjust, unethical or nonsensical rules. It's the only way things have ever been changed ☺'

Minor misdemeanours

One Villager, Gavin Fish, had some wise words on differentiating between major and minor issues:

'We should pardon "almost anything", once! Any parent/educator can apply the rules, the wise ones know what are the exceptions to the rules. We should not forget what we got up to when younger.

'There are no consequences this time, you need to do the work, it does carry a warning, next time my response will be different. I would rather you sorted this out for yourself, than that I have to be part of the solution. Decide for yourself that it is important and do it for that reason. On Strike One in Baseball you are still batting, another chance, it's just that the pressure is on, don't strike out.

'We as adults sometimes need to lighten up too. We don't have to respond to every single trespass, every misdemeanour. Sure that boy needs to shave (or whatever) but don't tell him in the same conversation where he is tearfully telling you about his domestic situation; overlook it. Yes, sometimes it is okay to turn a blind eye or to store it for a more receptive moment.

I did say I could pardon almost anything, but that doesn't include drugs, that is the 'almost' part. If you are corrupting yourself we help immediately, but if you are corrupting others by moving drugs on our premises, for that there is zero tolerance.

'Remember this, I will trust you until you give me reason not to. Keep my trust. When trust is broken it is regained with difficulty.'

Another take on teenage missteps and punishment comes from a Villager who was told by another Villager that she was teaching her kids they were allowed to break the law by allowing them to drink before the age of 18.

'I don't teach my kids to break laws but I'm also realistic,' said **Marysia Appleton**. 'My kids were never told to be good – I always told them that before they chose to be naughty to check the consequences and make sure they were happy to live with those, because whilst you will get away with things most of the time there is that percentage when you won't. As a result we used to have conversations about what school rules they intended to break 😬 My rule of life is that as long as whatever you do doesn't cause harm to life and the living, that as long as your actions are considerate and no one gets hurt – go for it. I know that's not mainstream but as I said before – I'd rather raise good kids than assholes.'

The hardest things

Chapter 6

CAN WE STILL WIN THE WAR AGAINST TECH?

Whatever aspect of family we have to consider as parents and guardians, we have an example from a previous generation of how we want to do something, what we'd like to avoid doing and how we feel we can improve. When it comes to parenting around the subject of smartphones and gaming – and all that is related to both of those things – we have just about zero historical fallback.

There is nothing in our own pre-parenting lives that prepared us for how far-reaching the advances in technology were going to be. Its tentacles have reached into the most intimate aspects of being human. We don't know how to anticipate the problems we'll have with our specific children and their individual relationships and engagement with tech.

We all have a screen problem

All the things a phone can do for you are human things that we need. We don't answer our phones so much as they answer our needs.

Our phones contain our people, our connections, our work, our bookshelf, our music, our radio, our camera, our compass, our maps, our weather, our time, our reminders, our links, our memories, our alarm, our schedules, our class updates, our group arrangements, our lists, our measuring tapes, our scanners, our meetings, our dictionaries, our encyclopaedia, our recipes, our exercise, our crosswords, our Sudoku.

Your phone is not a thing you can cut out of your life when its effects become problematic. We need phones. Our children need phones.

We can't just banish, ban or ignore them. We have to live with them.

We have to teach our children to live with them.

Aren't we all addicts?

If we're going to throw around 'addicted to your phone', we really will need to make sure that we are not being hypocritical.

We parents are very often glued to our phones. Yes, we need them for work and for coordinating domestic life, but what about those in-between times, when we are just sitting there listlessly judging some stranger's interiors or lusting after some fancy kitchen knife that will change our life forever.

Many of the reasons we have to engage with our phones are reasonable, but many are not. Often, we are on our phones out of habit, or because we have checked out from what's going on around us, or because our phones' many uses make them distracting: one minute you're checking the chances of rain, and the next minute you're googling 'Is Nicholas Cage still alive?' Sometimes we're on the phone because of exhaustion – mindless scrolling can be weirdly soothing when it all just gets a bit too much, and it requires only the movement of a thumb and our eyeballs.

So before we go labelling our children 'addicts' – which is quite a heavy word with lots of negative implications – we need to consider our own phone usage. Our children are often battling to get our attention as much as we're battling to get theirs.

As Villager **Julie Hall** points out, it's hard to ask someone to use their phone less when you don't.

Doctors do not agree on whether excessive phone time should be called an addiction. But we probably don't need doctors for us to spot problematic compulsivity and bad habits.

We just need to be sure we can recognise it in ourselves, too.

Villager **Gillian Viljoen** says, 'There is no one-size-fits-all approach to phones and it can be a lifeline for some of us.'

Let's break it down. A concerted scan of The Village posts yielded this summary:

The Good

- School communication – academics, extra-murals and homework instructions for our children
- Logistical communication between parents and children – all those changed plans schools can thrust on families
- Family communication – family groups are often a source of entertainment and a way of reminding its members of the humour and peculiarities that bind the group
- Friendship communication – social interaction is important for everyone, for us as parents communicating with our old tjommies from school and the new friends we make through our children, as well as for our children, who don't need to limit their interactions to times when they can see their friends in real life out of school
- Music! So much music! Playlists for long drives. Easy sharing. No one can be blamed for not putting the CDs back in their proper covers
- Artistic expression through photographing, drawing, journalling, videoing and recording
- Entertainment
- Research and fact-checking

- Reminders!
- Maps
- Easy sorting of information we want to hang on to
- Tracking for safety reasons – where our children are when they're out
- Checking in on our kids during a school day when they were worried about a test/feeling overwhelmed/had a tummy ache before school started.

With overuse, unconscious or out-of-control use of phones, there are some bad things that sneak in and become a way of life. Here are some of the ones The Villagers have expressed concerns about:

The Bad

- Bad posture
- Lack of necessary movement for growth and good health
- Constant notifications causing families to be interrupted in their conversation, which can lead to misunderstandings, irritation and disconnection from one another
- Avoidance of real-life difficulties
- Repeated hits to the user's confidence because of the comparison compulsion: everyone's lives, bodies, skin, wardrobe and holidays look so much better than your own
- Social isolation when solitary activities on the phone become easier than direct social interaction that requires listening and responding
- Increased stress, anxiety and depression
- Loss of sleep
- Lack of outside time, which leads to lack of contemplation, appreciation for the environment, Vitamin D, fresh air and, of course, movement, which is so necessary for so many aspects of health.

And then there are the truly worrying, desperation-stations, let's-hope-it-doesn't-happen-to-us things about smartphones.

The Ugly

- Bullying, often invisible to others, and a particular risk for people with depression
- Abuse
- Grooming
- Vulnerability to flattery and hence to solicitation of compromising photographs
- Vulnerability to financial abuse (one Village's younger child accidentally spent R28 000 on games)
- Easy exposure to pornography
- Accidents.

'The mere presence of a phone'

One of the breakthrough studies into the effects of phones on our lives showed that 'The mere presence of one's own smartphone reduces available cognitive capacity' (that was the actual title of the study). The study showed that even if a person's phone was on silent, upside down on the desk beside them, or in a bag or pocket near them, they scored lower on cognitive tests than when the phone was in a different room altogether.

'Screentime' or 'screen-free time'?

Phones can be disruptive in ways that irritate even ourselves. You find yourself having picked the phone up 'quickly' to check the load-shedding schedule, only to burn the onions. Or you get up in the night to go to the loo, check the time on your phone and the next minute you're looking at videos of cake decoration.

Screentime, whether we like it or not, is pretty much 'all the time'.

Phones can be used in so many helpful ways that we don't even notice the slow creep of phone numbness. We don't notice how much time we're pouring into the screen without any measurable returns, except maybe a stiff neck and a few low-key dopamine hits from doggie or dance content.

There are numerous requests on The Village from parents asking other parents what the appropriate amount of screentime is for children of certain ages, and people offer their own solutions, but it's hard to extrapolate guidelines – even from studies – because of the fact that teenagers need access to their phones in the same way that we need access to ours.

What seems to make more sense is to flip the idea of 'how much screentime' to 'non-negotiable screen-free times'. For many families, this is at the table, and it includes phones being on silent so that no one gets distracted from the business of family eating together.

Many Villagers have a rule of no phones before school. How else would you get everyone out the door on time? Hard enough without phones in the mix.

A very sensible practice that many Villagers apply is for teenagers not to have their phones in their rooms at night. Parents who did this reported that the most common objections to this rule were: 'I need the alarm' and 'I need music to fall asleep'. The solution: get an old-fashioned battery-operated cheapo alarm, and a Bluetooth speaker that can work over distance.

Any other reasons for needing a phone in the night are probably not very good ones.

Based on the scientific evidence of 'the mere presence of your phone', it is probably just as well that many Villagers have rules about where the phones are during homework, study and exam times.

When you really need to concentrate, study or spend quality time with other people, phones out of sight and on silent are a common-

sense way to live. A conscious decision to remove smartphones to other rooms so that important aspects of life can continue and flourish is a baseline requirement for life for many Villagers, and most online articles on the topic of screens in families agree that all families should have:
- Smartphone-free hours
- Web-free times
- TV- and game-free times
- Web-free spaces in the home.

The parents who seem to have the least stress about their children's cell phone usage are the ones in whose homes usage is negotiated. **Gillian Viljoen** had this to say: 'Usually we decide together as a family. For example, we like to choose a series we can 'listen to' and still play on our phones as a relaxing pastime. When we want to watch a movie we want to focus on, and phone use will irritate others, we discuss and ask.

'When my son was about 12/13, we negotiated a rule to put his phone in my room at bedtime. We came to the conclusion together. He struggles with sleep and the blue-tick-must-respond problems started. Also being informed about homework at 10pm from a WhatsApp group. Both caused extreme stress.

'There were several toxic WhatsApp group experiences during those years, which were the foundation for discussions.'

Vanessa says

When it comes to all things screen-related, we turn to Sarah Hoffman and Pam Tudin-Buchalter, aka Klikd. They are great friends of The Village, a lawyer and psychologist growing good digital humans.

Pam and Sarah say ✓

There is no one formula to getting the online world right with our screenagers but there are some golden nuggets that make the ride on the digital highway a whole lot smoother – our top 11 tips for parenting the teen digital native:

- *Nugget 1: **You can't be held hostage in your own home.** You are the boss parent and you have to own it, claim and eat it alive for breakfast, lunch and supper. If they feel you waver on the boundaries they will find the gap and play it every time.*
- *Nugget 2: **They will look for porn and porn will look for them.** Be ready to have open and honest, non-judgemental conversations about porn.*
- *Nugget 3: **No phones in the bedroom at night.** Choose the phone's bedtime and then get it to dock in the kitchen. If you have a sneaky teen, dock it in your own bedroom. Over 80% of the dangerous stuff happens online at night.*
- *Nugget 4: **No one is immune to digital distraction – not even the smartest among them.** Our teens hold this idea that somehow they can study, reply to a girlfriend's text and watch a movie all while handing in a good essay on Napoleon's flaws as a leader. The endless pings and dings drive us to distraction, so we know they're affecting them too! Find the middle ground. Use apps that allow them to hear from two of their besties while all others are muted (such as Focus Mode on iOS devices). This removes the FOMO factor but keeps you in the moderate parent zone. Being a reasonable parent with a teen builds trust and allows them to grow autonomy and accountability.*
- *Nugget 5: **Step out of the power struggle.** The device seems to have a built-in button that says 'fight over me'. Don't. Establish your family values and calmly hold to them. Words like 'That is not how this family rolls, so no, we don't have the*

device at the table' help our teens to feel like they belong to something bigger than whatever the device is offering in the moment. The trick is to set up a contract repeatedly over time for device use. It's a moving beast and our children mature. Let them grow into the responsibility.

- *Nugget 6: It's never too late to set the ground rules.* You as the parent are always free to say, 'I've been thinking, I want us to relook at how we all use our devices at home. Can we agree on x or y going forward?' Make sure you recognise that the contract is reciprocal. Let them ask for some things too: 'Mom, stop posting pics of me on Facebook!' has to be honoured. In this way everyone has some skin in the game.
- *Nugget 7: Don't be threatened by AI.* They are going to embrace it and so should we! We all know that ChatGPT has altered the education landscape forever, but we promise there is much good in it too. There are plenty of ways AI can and does enhance critical thinking. Use it together and have fun with it!
- *Nugget 8: If you don't connect with them, AI will.* Many of our teens are also turning to AI for therapeutic support. Snapchat has a built-in AI therapist now so they don't even have to leave their favourite platform to access it. At Klikd, we tried it, and there's no denying that the feedback on how to deal with some tricky social dynamics was pretty sound. But human connection trumps all. Again, embrace what is while staying connected: 'What did AI come up with on this front? Did you think it was good advice? What doesn't it get?' Talk, talk, talk, even when they are rolling their eyes.
- *Nugget 9: Always start chats about any topic to do with screens and teen/tween behaviour from the 'world out there'.* Come from a place of curiosity, not judgement. This means talking about how they see the behaviour of others 'out there' in their school, then perhaps learners in their grade

and then bring it in a little closer to their friend group before tackling them about their own behaviour. When the conversation is going really well, you can get personal and ask directly about their own online behaviour. But this takes time and will require your children to really trust that you are wanting to listen and hear, not judge and correct.

- *Nugget 10: No one is immune to being caught by an online predator. Every teen thinks they are immune to some of the online dangers (and scams) that surface over and over again. They are not. In particular, they think that somehow they will be the one to outsmart the predator lurking in chat forums or pretending to be a bestie they met on rugby tour. But even our smartest, coolest, sportiest screenagers get whacked out of left field. Chat about examples at the dinner table. Ask them who they know who has been caught out. How did it go down? Listen without judgement, show curiosity. Just the talking helps them to be more vigilant. Lecturing? Well, they are deaf to the lecture.*
- *Nugget 11: Always be the soft landing place. Online mistakes are going to happen. Be the soft landing place for your t(w)eens when they mess up online. Huge, dramatic overreactions and fury only send one message: 'I can't tell my parents anything – they are just going to rage.' It pushes everything underground and pretty much ensures that our kids tell their friends (or worse, no one) when mistakes happen.*

We are not saying no to consequences for messing up online (be it online bullying, sending a nude, forwarding porn). We are just saying, choose the order. First, have their backs. Later, when you have heard the story and the feelings that come with it, look at ways to respond to the misdemeanour.

Consider saying things like, 'I'm going to listen first and let you tell me your version of the whole story. I promise I won't interrupt'. Or, 'It's okay to tell me something you think is hard for me to hear'. Or, 'I'm not saying I won't be disappointed or maybe even angry, but I am going to be your mom/dad first'.

There is plenty good to be found online. Exposure to information, communities, support, culture, political groups are good things in any teen world. We sought them out as teens too; the fact that they're online doesn't mean they're all bad. So many of our teens are finding healthy, like-minded people to grow their ideas, create change and make a better world. Let them! The more we fight them about the devices, the more it all happens away from us. Then we'll never get to hear what they are really passionate about, thinking of doing, wanting to make happen.

And remember, screentime should never be about 'how much' time. It really should be measured against how they are managing all the important bits in their lives – exercise, real-time connection with friends, homework, chores at home. When those are in place, we are happy for them to be on their devices for some downtime. If one falls by the wayside, quietly make the observation and give them a week to rectify. If they can't get it right, simply say, 'We are going to hold the phone until you get your balance back.' They don't always love it, but they get it. Most importantly, it keeps you out of the power struggle and the screaming matches.

Ultimately, there's lots to be worry about and lots to celebrate when it comes to these darn devices. Our kids hear the important messages about device use when we go in lightly, repeatedly, in different and curious ways. Asking them what they think the potential mental health concerns, dangers and risks are, and really letting them have their view about different social media issues, is where victory lies. Chatting at the table, asking them what they notice in their friends, in us as parents – and then, later, asking them about themselves – gives them space to really think about the issues, instead of fighting us in every round.

Vanessa says

Ouch. Another area of parenting where, as responsible adults, we have to role model good behaviour. If we can't put our own devices down, we can't expect our offspring to do so either. Sorry! I know this is tough (to be honest, I can't even say no to second helpings of roast potatoes, let alone stop doom-scrolling through Instagram reels). But no one said parenting was easy. IMHO, the best antidote to any form of addiction is busyness ... and community. If you want to get yourself, or your child, off a screen, get them and yourself interested in something else. Encourage other hobbies or activities, and be actively present and supportive of them. If they don't have hobbies, get them volunteering, working, learning or active, with you or without you.

Being otherwise occupied may not mean that kids spend less of their downtime off their screens, but it will mean less downtime, alone, to sink into the abyss. And busyness is the path to a more rewarding experience in the real world. Loneliness makes a child more vulnerable to all the ills society can throw at them, including the numbing power of screens.

Chapter 7

THINGS THAT GO BUMP IN THE NIGHT

So much about being the parent of teenagers cannot be anticipated. But the one thing we know we must expect – even if we haven't accepted it consciously – is that having a teenager means that sex has entered the home.

Teenagers 'have' sex in all the glorious and inglorious ways that sex exists, from thought-sex and dream-sex and inexplicable longings, all the way through to obsessive masturbation, anal sex and blowjobs for buddies.

Parents thinking about their children having sex can be as cringey and awful as children imagining their parents having sex. Even though we know sex is part of the teenage deal, we prefer to think of our sweet little kids in their beloved holey Spiderman suits or ragged tutus, sweetly drawing pictures of us without necks and eyebrows. We don't really want to think of them as grown-up-ish enough to want to investigate someone else's mouth with their tongues.

We just don't want to think about them much that way because it partly means acknowledging that they are growing away from us. And if their sexuality makes itself known before we expected it to, at the age of say 12 or 13, then it's not just a huge surprise – it can be a full body blow to even the most liberal-minded.

One Village mother wrote about how her 17-year-old son couldn't find his Speedo and swimming cap so she tried to help him. While digging in his tog bag, she found five condoms, three of which were used. She had prepared him for sex. They'd spoken about consent, STDs, respect and 'basically everything under the sun that I felt was necessary to make good choices'. Yet the condoms shocked her. And then she was shocked by her shock. It was only noon and she was ready to open a bottle of wine.

As **Yvonne Rabeling** pointed out: 'I suppose as parents we are all shocked to some degree when we find out our children are having sex.'

Karin says

Why are we so shocked?

Here's my theory: it's a rude awakening.

Nothing makes you more aware of the lostness of your offspring's childhood than the sprouting of adult hairs on what was once the silkiest of chinny-chin-chins. They might have sassed you, slammed a door in anger, or handled a tricky social situation in a very mature way at some point between consuming only milk and now, but none of those things fully prepares you for tiny breasts pressing against an outgrown T-shirt.

'It's always a shock,' wrote **Sherry Japha** about one parent's disbelief at discovering her son was sexually active, 'to realise our kids are growing up faster than we realised'.

But apart from realising that this is it for the 'child' years, coming face to face with your child's sexuality is the opening of a floodgate of implications about what this means.

Sex is kak-complicated. It shouldn't be. But it is.

Firstly, we all have our own sex baggage. We seldom have a straightforward relationship with our own sexuality and, if we do now, we probably had to outgrow all kinds of ideas in order to get there. We are plagued by abuse from our childhood, complicated messaging about what our genitals are there for, rejection, body worries, cultural expectation and judgement, morality issues, rape, rape culture and power imbalances, sexual assault and – so very often – shame in some form or another.

Our children are a little less burdened in the sense that we live in different times so they're more open, which is another reason we can get tied up in knots of awkwardness about their sexuality.

For many of us parents of teenagers, we never had conversations about sex with our folks. Maybe not because of religious or moralistic reasons, but because of a general haze around sex. It just didn't exist in the world the way that exams, family braais and picking up the dog poo did. Sex was what we broached with friends, and most of us both questioned and spoke from extreme ignorance in a world in which there was no sex education.

If we were extremely unlucky, on the other hand, we learnt about sex from adults in a way that no one should learn about sex from adults: through experience.

The point is, back when we were turning into hormone rockets, adults were adults, and we were us, and the divisions were clear. No one acknowledged our ignorance, their silence or the plain fact that sex really is as completely ordinary as KFC and covering exercise books in brown paper and plastic every January.

Our kids, on the other hand – either because we refused to endorse the silence, or because information is easier to come by now, or because sex education is *actually taught* at school – want to talk about sex, and often do talk to us about sex. It can be awkward as hell all around, but it's a lot better than the hush-hush so many of us grew up with.

Since most of us never received a formal sex education, we're often lagging on knowledge beyond our own experience. A good place to start is with some facts and definitions.

What the law says about age and sex

A child is a person under 18. That means that if your child turns 18 in Grade 11 and starts to engage in consensual sex with one or several partners, they are entitled to.

The age of consent is the age at which a child in South Africa, regardless of their gender or sexual orientation, can give their consent to engage in sexual activities. In South Africa, that age is 16. Anyone who has sex with someone who is younger than 16 is engaging in a crime.

An exception to the age of consent is that if children between the ages of 12 and 16 are engaging in sexual acts together, they will not be criminally charged.

Another exception to the age of consent is that it is not criminal for a child older than 12 to have sex with a partner who is less than two years older than they are.

Sexual activity with someone under the age of 12 is statutory rape or sexual assault. A child under the age of 12 cannot give consent to have sex.

Consent is the clear, unmistakable and voluntary agreement between people to participate in a sexual activity. This includes all sexual acts. You cannot consent to sex if you are asleep or under the influence of alcohol or drugs. That means sex with a drunk person is non-consensual sex. Even if they have said yes to sex, if they are drunk, their 'Yes' is not considered consent. Further, a person may change their mind even after giving consent – even during the act – which means that the consent is withdrawn.

One Villager posted that her daughter had been drunk and a boy the family knows had sex with her. She was too drunk to fully know what was going on or to say no. The mother was wondering about next steps. Another Villager, **Amanda Williamson**, gave a succinct declaration on the matter: 'It's rape. If a person is intoxicated, they are not able to give consent. This boy needs to know that. At the very least, his parents should be informed. It is not your daughter's fault.

She made a common teen mistake and had some drinks. The boy raped her.'

The 'age of consent' and 'consent' are not the same thing. The age of consent is the age at which people are considered to be able to make decisions about with whom and how they engage in sexual activity. **Being of the age of consent does not mean automatically consenting to sex. Consent** means agreeing to specific sexual activity in a specific moment with a specific person, and it can be withdrawn, even during sexual activity. As one Villager put it, 'As a schoolteacher, I teach enthusiastic consent. An enthusiastic yes. Anything less that that is a no. Consent can be withdrawn at any point.'

Starting the sex conversation

An anonymous Villager asked how and when Villager parents approached the birds-and-bees conversation. She had a ten-year old asking loads of questions and who was showing definite physical signs of puberty.

'He knows everything about how babies are born but he doesn't know about the actual deed, as in sexual intercourse.' He also didn't know about masturbation.

'I'm dreading [the conversation] ... we haven't told him mainly because all his friends also don't talk or know and parents in my friends' groups think it is too young. I don't want my child to be the one that tells all the boys in his group.'

She said he was so irritable one day that she asked him what was wrong, and he said it felt like there was a storm inside him. She thought it had to be hormones.

'I don't just want to buy a book, but would like to have a meaningful conversation with him.'

Another Villager answered that she'd had 'the basic talk with all my kids at 10 years'. She spoke about masturbation as normal and nothing to be ashamed of. She and her husband made themselves available to answer questions and, as the years went on, the answers became more detailed 'but age appropriate'. Their pocket money includes reminders to buy protection.

'In my opinion,' she wrote, 'start the conversation – keep it open, be direct and honest [while] keeping it age appropriate.'

A bunch of useful advice from the group

'Start with biology. Use a pen and paper. The questions will move from the biology to emotions and he will cry out "Stop, yuk!" when the info goes beyond what he needs.' – **Caroline Calburn**

'When they ask a question answer completely honestly. The biggest thing for me was teaching my children to have a huge and abundant dose of self-respect.' – **Raffaella Wainer**

'My children always knew, thanks to my wise mother who had a traumatic sex talk with her parents at age 11, knowing absolutely nothing before that. She vowed it would never happen to her children, and the story, coupled with the facts, conversations and chats, have been inherited by her grandchildren. It really doesn't have to be a dreaded chore or something shameful. We pass on all those unspoken attitudes and nuances in our nonverbal communication. We honestly need to get over ourselves. Our children's sexual health depends on it. As a doula, I have seen time and again how negative sexual health [messaging] like shame, embarrassment, fear and any kind of negative experience shows up at the birth. Positive, joyful and open conversations and attitudes about sex from a very early age are a gift to our children, our future grandchildren and hopefully even theirs.' – **Lisl van den Hoven**

'When my twins asked me how babies were made I said, "I don't want to tell you," so of course they were all intrigued and asked why, so I said, "Because you'll laugh". Which made them laugh and set the tone for a funny, interactive conversation that covered all the topics they wanted to know about and more. And I think they know

now that I can take anything they ask in my stride and with humour.'
– **Michelle Cowie**

'I bought an amazing book for my son as I am a single mom in a same-sex relationship (now) called "How willies work and other interesting facts". Hilarious and factual.' – **Zunia Boucher-Myers**

Privacy and boundaries

This Villager was navigating the balance between her kid's privacy with her concerns over her mental safety:

'I was missing one of my special kitchen plates. I asked my daughter (20) whether it was in her room. She denied it, but considering the state of her room and that half the kitchen crockery ends up in her room I wasn't sure how sure she was. Anyway, after asking all the other children and [our domestic worker] and looking everywhere I asked her again. Denial. A few days later I decided to have a look myself. Needless to say I found it in a drawer, with dagga pips in it. But with a pink vibrator on top of the plate and dagga pips! I really didn't know what to do! I wanted my plate, I needed to address the dagga pips, but didn't want to have to give away that I was going through her drawers and certainly didn't want her to know that I know about the vibrator!

'We'd had many drug talks over the years and maybe naively I didn't think and still don't really think she would be a user. (She suffers from anxiety and she is in agreement that meds, coffee, drugs, alcohol mess with her head and she is cautious. I even got microdoses of psilocybin for her once and she stopped taking it as she felt it made things worse. We also have a friend whose son's life was ruined w[ith] drugs and another whose son developed schizophrenia after becoming a dagga user. She is well aware of these examples). I think the dagga was brought to her room by a friend.

'Nonetheless I still wanted to address it with her and reinforce the message. (And maybe she had put her toe in the dagga water, who knows ...)

'But I'm not such a cool mum that I could skip over the vibrator without blushing, and her privacy in this matter was certainly violated and rightfully she could have been very angry w[ith] me.

'It was around the time the Thai boys were stuck in that cave. It was a story we all followed closely. I used it as an opener and I told her with genuine tears in my eyes how worried I always am about her. And specially so because of her condition. And how bad drugs and specially dagga could be for her. She reassured me she wouldn't take drugs. And as a PS to our conversation asked her again whether she had seen my missing plate!

'Every time I got home I'd check whether the plate was back in the cupboard and every time it wasn't and there was a new development around the boys in the cave I would have the same conversation with her, becoming more and more emotional. Probably about 5 times!

'And on the day the boys starting coming out of the cave, my plate appeared in the cupboard! Along with lots of tears, love and hugs from my daughter as we celebrated. I think the penny dropped for her that I knew and she knew I was saving her the embarrassment of the discovery of the vibrator. Parenting young adults, eish!'

Vanessa says

Ask yourself this question (if you can bear to!): do you want your teen to grow up to have a happy, empowered sex life, with no guilt or shame?

I'd like to hope that, as much as we are able to think about it without vomiting, that is what all loving parents will aim for, once we have overcome our squeamishness around the subject.

If you do want your kids to grow up to be relaxed and healthy around the subject of sex, you have no choice: as their parent, somewhere around the time they turn 15 or 16, you have to get out of their heads – and that means you have to get out of their bedrooms.

Another easier-said-than-done? Of course. No news there!

Our own parents may have not been as enlightened or pragmatic. My father told me, at 22, that as a woman, with regards to sexual experience, I was like a car. (Interesting!) As soon as I had been 'used', he said, my value would drop, like a car once it's driven out of the showroom.

Ha. I told him that I had lost my virginity six years previously and had at least done him the favour of choosing, for my first partner, a nice Jewish medical student. Suffice to say we have never spoken about my sex life since then. Which is exactly as it should be, in my opinion.

Facing the fact that our children have a sex life of any description can be excruciating for a parent, indicating, as it does, that our time as No. 1 in their life is well and truly over. The double whammy? Our moppet is now adult enough to have discovered what their sexual organs are there for.

Speaking as a rather more conventional mom than I expected to be, the firmly closed door, strange sounds and endless empty bottles of body lotion and tissues in the bin were the shocking and confronting signal that my babies had grown up much sooner than I was ready for. Are parents ever *ready? Too bad if we're not. If our teens are, we'd better be! Because our rules, regulations and punishments are no match for a teenager's hormones. And there's an excellent chance that our rules, regulations and punishments could cause damage for years, making no positive contribution to the outcome we hope for at all.*

Teenagers have sex. Whether we can stomach it or not.

Tell them that they can't do 'it' in 'your house'? They'll do it somewhere else.

Tell them that sex is only for marriage? They'll do it anyway.

Tell them they're not ready to have sex? They'll still do it. (Yes, even your precious little angel – at it like a piston.)

Tell them your religion forbids sex? They'll feel wracked with guilt and judgement about it, and do it anyway. (Ask anyone who attended a Catholic school or was dragged to the NG Kerk on Sundays).

Tell them having sex makes them 'cheap'? They'll feel cheap ... and still do it.

Say nothing? According to recent studies, the average boy first encounters sexual content (porn) at the age of about 11. If you don't deal with it, porn will be their education.

Enforce a past generation's values and rules on a young adult and you are pretty much guaranteed the slammed door of secrecy and the evaporation of your most precious tool for navigating the relationship: open lines of communication.

For a youngster, being able to ask questions and share secrets and fears with their parents, on any subject, is a bedrock of security and love. They may not want to, but the security comes from knowing they can. The trick, it seems, is to tell them enough to enable them to feel comfortable and informed ... and then step back and let them get on with it, without shame or judgement.

A friend of mine's lovely husband took each of his three boys out to dinner, when the time came, and told them to ask him anything. They did. Mine would have cringed and thrown up into their hamburgers. I told my children, 'Listen. Do whatever feels good with your own body, but do it in private. If you ever need to ask me about anything that is worrying you, I'll answer.' And, 'Never do anything to anyone else without asking, "Is this okay with you?" and obeying their answer.' I asked them if they needed to know about confusing impulses, STDs and contraception. I provided condoms surreptitiously and washed truckloads of bed linen without comment. I've let partners sleep over and feel welcome at breakfast the next day.

Not always easy. I promise.

But ... it's your beloved person's body. Their life. Their business, after all.

And consensual, happy sex is natural and healthy. Lest we forget, our job as parents remains to give them the foundation to discover 'happy' and 'healthy' for themselves. And then to head back to the sidelines.

Chapter 8

EVERYONE IN BETWEEN

It feels like just five minutes ago that girls were girls and boys were boys and the only confusing thing we needed to ponder was that sometimes girls liked girls and boys liked boys.

Now, boys can be girls and girls can be boys and boys and girls can decide to be neither or both at the same time. Or to sometimes be one and sometimes the other.

Boys can wear dresses and heels and shave their hairy armpits, and not be gay, and girls can keep their armpits hairy and kiss thems and theys, and will roll their eyes at you if you want to know what this *means*, bloody hell. Does it mean they're a lesbian? We don't mind. We just want to understand, we try to tell them.

And while we're asking questions, what is a pansexual? Does a trans man become a cis man through gender correction surgery or does being trans turn you into another gender but trans can never be cis or cis be trans? If no doctor fiddles with the nethers, but the girl we once knew starts shaving their face, is they, are she, is he, a man now?

Wait, what is cis?

And is it okay to even ask these questions because man (can we say that?), people get so cross if you ask a question!

Binders and puberty blockers and what are your pronouns and

what do you mean what are my pronouns? Where are the overlaps between sexual attraction, sex, gender, sexual expression and sexual and gender identity? What is meant by fluidity, non-binary, gender queer. How many letters are there in the LGBT alphabet?

We parents are really trying hard, but WT entire F is going on and how are we ever going to understand it, let alone have a solid, unshakable opinion about something that is so, well, fluid and sensitive?

And mainly: is this a fad we can just grit our teeth through?

One of our Villagers had the wisest take on all these questions that came bubbling out of a distraught parent:

'As an adult, I also find it difficult to understand but I know that I do not need to understand to be able to have grace towards others, so I will learn and respect.' – **Tillie Smith**

Luckily, The Village has at least one trans parent we know of, one trans health professional and dozens of parents of trans teens. They all help us navigate the choppy waters of our generational differences, and our biological, scientific and anthropological ignorance. From their own experiences, they come back bearing gifts of wisdom and insight for all Villagers who haven't yet had the opportunity to think about the meaning of gender.

When **Nikki Stuart-Thompson Hyde** needed 'ways to address gender and normalise the understanding of non-binary identities with my young kids', The Village showed heart and encouragement.

She wrote: 'As we all keep learning about how to be more inclusive and to treat people with proper respect and consideration, including the use of proper pronouns, I am conscious of having to unlearn what I thought I knew and to re-learn. I think it is so important to make sure our young kids are exposed to more enlightened thinking and understanding from the beginning. I am just not sure where to start. From such a young age, everything is about he or she and gender norms, and I just want to make sure that they learn more than this. This is not about their own journeys yet, but just about making sure their minds stay open before society closes them down.'

A lot of the responses she received were also good advice for parents who wanted to educate themselves.

Karen Jeynes is a Villager people often tag in discussions on gender. One of her suggestions to Nikki was to start with Sam Killerman's Genderbread Person:

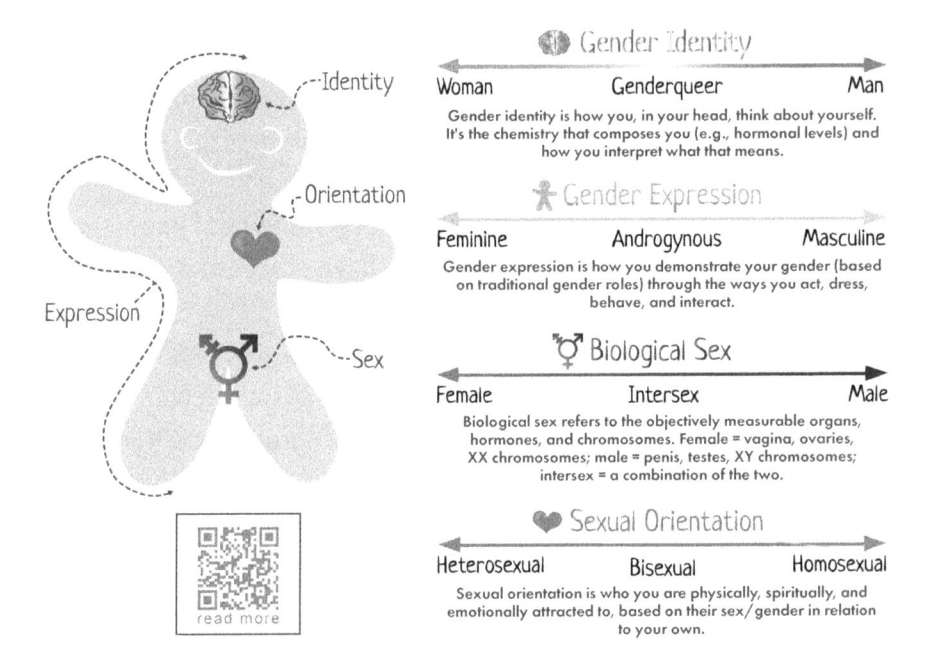

Gender Identity

Woman — Genderqueer — Man

Gender identity is how you, in your head, think about yourself. It's the chemistry that composes you (e.g., hormonal levels) and how you interpret what that means.

Gender Expression

Feminine — Androgynous — Masculine

Gender expression is how you demonstrate your gender (based on traditional gender roles) through the ways you act, dress, behave, and interact.

Biological Sex

Female — Intersex — Male

Biological sex refers to the objectively measurable organs, hormones, and chromosomes. Female = vagina, ovaries, XX chromosomes; male = penis, testes, XY chromosomes; intersex = a combination of the two.

Sexual Orientation

Heterosexual — Bisexual — Homosexual

Sexual orientation is who you are physically, spiritually, and emotionally attracted to, based on their sex/gender in relation to your own.

The Genderbread Person was designed by Sam Killermann to explain in the simplest terms what the difference is between gender identity, gender expression, biological sex and sexual expression. www.ItsPronouncedMetrosexual.com

Karen also suggested the following:

1. 'Are you bringing examples of gender diversity into their lives, from your friends to the media you consume?
2. How do you play with your kids? Are their toys/games gendered? When you play pretend games, is it gender diverse? On a simpler level, when my family played The Game Of Life, we'd choose different gendered characters to our genders at the time, have same-sex couples and so on.
3. Make sure your compliments aren't gendered.

4. Use the news/current affairs to start conversations eg. Mentioning that it's cool that a trans athlete won an Olympic medal.
5. Normalise using they/them pronouns for people whose gender you don't know or where it is irrelevant eg. 'My colleague was sad today cos their dog was sick.' No gender needed.
6. My main advice is always opening up to your kids about stuff so that they in turn will open up to you. So a simple thing like "You know, growing up, I was taught that women always have to wear make-up, but honestly I don't always feel like wearing it and that's ok" can open up conversation about gender and what it means.'

Nicky Kingwell shared this: 'As the mom of a transgender child we are walking this journey. To date, my child's school has been amazing. The kids were taken through this book [*I am Jazz*, by Jazz Jennings], and there is absolute acceptance and openness. It's really the normalising of transgender that is needed. One of the things through our journey that our psychologist taught us is that kids just need to be exposed to different and new situations in a safe environment, where they trust the adults that are guiding them. That's why schools and parents tackling these issues with their kids head on is so important, and in a very matter of fact age appropriate way.'

Is this my fault?

'This is one of the hardest things I've ever shared,' an anonymous Villager wrote when she said her daughter, who had said she was bisexual, was now reading up about being trans. The single mom wanted to know what she'd done wrong and whether her child's ADHD, lack of masculine role models, or an alcoholic father might have 'pushed her to this'.

To which **Carle Dehning** replied: 'You haven't failed, your child spoke to you. All you can do is listen and love. So much can happen as your child finds their path. See this as an opportunity to bond closer with your child by letting them. Know you love her unconditionally. She may remain exactly as she is, or she may change, but be assured that changes don't happen overnight. If she is trans, it is a long road before big changes happen. If she isn't trans, she may identify as gender neutral or gender fluid. Or she may just be hating puberty. #beenthere'

In response to the anonymous mother's worry about what had 'caused' her child's questioning, a Villager shared that she'd struggled to have children and then had twins, one born female and one male (the terms for this are AFAB and AMAB, meaning 'assigned female/male at birth', based on genitalia at birth). Her AFAB child told her that they were actually trans.

She wrote: 'I was happy for him and supported him fully. But inside my heart was grieving. I was grieving for the loss of the child my daughter was. But after a short while, I realised I hadn't lost the person my child was. He was exactly the same person on the inside, the same kind, gentle, loving, caring person. He was just different on the outside. In fact, he was even better than before because he was happier within himself. So, I understand your worry and your fears. If you child does decide to go ahead with this journey, you will not lose them. They are still the same person on the inside, just different on the outside.'

Is all this gender and sexuality questioning just a fad?

Learning that a child is wondering whether they might be queer is very upsetting for some parents, usually out of concern that their child is going to have a tough life but sometimes for less loving reasons (my child is not what I want them to be/this is morally wrong/this is a ridiculous fad that they've fallen for).

The parents of queer Village kids assure us, over and over again, that this is not a crisis, that things will unfold as they unfold, and that our main job, despite our worries, is to be supportive and non-judgemental: 'I'm posting this anonymously to protect my child – and in reply to the recent discussions here about gender/sexuality/body dysphoria – I apologize for the length but please read if you want to be or have been part of the conversation. I am mother to a 16 yo trans boy – he has socially transitioned at his school from when he was about 5 years old – he knew he was a boy from when he was two. With the recent alarming developments in the US and many African countries following suit to take back and even criminalize health/medical care for trans youth – I would like to comment on a few misconceptions that I noticed in some of the posts: my child has been on puberty blockers since the age of 11 – prescribed by an endocrinologist and supported by psychologists – had he not been given that opportunity we would have forced him to experience female puberty, periods and breast development which would have been the cause for severe body dysphoria and trauma – imagine if you are a woman you wake up tomorrow in a male body – how confusing and scary would that be – even for an adult – to put a child through this is cruel to say the least.

'Puberty blockers are reversible – their function is 'buying time' for a child who might still realize in the years to come that they do not wish to medically transition for a number of reasons – they might be non-binary or gender fluid or they simply do not want to go the medical route – in some cases they come to understand that they are not trans and their body discomfort was not so much about gender but sexual identity. Sometimes there are underlying causes such as sexual abuse or mental health issues which a good psychologist will be able to see.

'Nobody gives blockers to a child on a whim – there is a difference between kids experimenting with different identities as they should during puberty (and we need to respect all of those too by the way) – or a child expressing anguish and distress about their assigned gender and body. In my child's case it was very early and clear – other kids take longer, a lot of the time they just want to fit in and try to be what society tells them they should be ... at a cost to their well being.

'The narrative that this is some newfangled craziness that only leads to pronoun confusion and chaos at schools is dangerous and wrong. The fact that we see so many more kids with gender "confusion" is not a new "phenomenon" – gender has always been on a spectrum, and there were always people/children who have felt they didn't fit into the binary and/or felt wrong in their bodies but could never express this before – and as a result ended up depressed or even suicidal. The fact that we now have more knowledge and language around these issues – that we have options to deal with them in the best interest of our children – is a good thing. And yes it means that more and more children will be able to voice their concerns, confusion and feelings about their gender identity – and yes it is confusing for us parents too – believe me I wished so many times we didn't have to go through all of this and could just be 'normal'. But normal is only what any given society prescribes and our old normal was based on misinformation about gender as a biological fact – it is not – gender is a social construct – there is amazing research/articles out there that explain it much better than I can.

'Bottom line: my child has decided to medically transition at 14 after 3 years of blockers – which means he is now also on cross hormones – which is an irreversible process as far as his fertility goes. We "allowed" this with the support of our endocrinologist and psychologists as my child had been consistent in his identity since the age of three and all he wanted was to be able to experience puberty like the other boys his age. At 16 he couldn't be happier. He won't have to have surgery as many of his peers who were not given the options of blockers – or who only realized during or after puberty that they were trans. There are so many trans kids in this country – especially in the rural areas – who suffer silently – whose body dysphoria leads to self harm – they are forced to use binders that are restrictive and painful, if they even have access to mental health facilities they are put on anti depressants, some are suicidal. Helping those children would not be difficult – but there is stigma, misinformation and of course limited access to resources

'For those of us who are lucky enough to have access to information and medical resources – It is not too much to ask to learn new things and to expand our horizons to include everyone as they are even if that means we have to learn new terms, struggle with changing pronouns and new names – it's a small price to pay in my opinion – and doesn't hurt anyone … life is hard enough for our kids – let's show them what love and acceptance look like – so they can become the loving and accepting adults we all want them to be … Thank you for reading'.

Gender-affirming treatment does not begin with a scalpel

Many parents seem to believe, wrongly, that 'being trans' means immediately getting surgery, which is a frightening thought because surgery is always frightening, even if it is for removing an appendix. Surgery, though, is a much later step in a long process. Many trans people never have gender-affirming surgery at all. One Villager gave this explanation:

'Hey there Lovely Village.

'I thought I'd just check in here to give you a different view in light of recent Transgender posts.

'I'm a mum to a beautiful tween daughter (AMAB – assigned male at birth).

'At the age of 3 she started wearing dresses and begging for long hair and pink nails.

'This wasn't a life we knew anything about so we started therapy for her early on in life to make sure she was always comfortable within herself and being authentic.

'Suppressing your true self is never a good idea.

'No surprises here but she ended up, at age 10 asking us to call her she, changed into a girl's uniform and we've supported her all the way.

'She is on puberty blockers to prevent boy puberty (this is completely reversible for those who don't know that).

'It doesn't come easily.

'It's a process.

'Doctors don't just fill in script and off you go.

'There are many steps in order to go this route.

'But to put it simply, it buys you time and delays puberty.

'Which for people who need this, is absolutely life changing.

'We all know teenagers are all over the show, we all know they can't decide what meal they want, never mind what gender they think they want to be.

'However, understandably some may think this is "a new fad".

'A couple of things on that:

1. It only appears new because it's more visible and more acceptable, which is exactly as it should be.
2. There is no person who would, on a whim, actively choose this life for themselves; it's expensive, it's full of judgement, it's hard, very very hard. Only the bravest of human beings live their authentic selves despite the world being against them.

'I know for a fact, going through puberty as a boy would have killed my child.

'We have, thanks to medical intervention, given her a chance to live.

'Not all people need this step as some are still undecided, but if they do, it's imperative to their happiness.

'It's important to recognise that every single journey is different.

'It's a spectrum.

'Ranging from one extreme to the next and everything in between, so one person's story will vary to the next, but respect and inclusion is always a good idea.

'My last thought on this.

'There are so many "different" ways of being, if it doesn't affect you, then don't let it bother you.

'There is no single child who will be swayed to be Trans if they aren't truly so.

'It's not contagious ☺.

'Be kind.

'Be inclusive.

'Keep your eye on the prize, which is simply to set our kids up for a happy future.

'No matter what.

'Love a Mum to the most courageous and beautiful child I've ever known.'

Vanessa says

I ask for empathy, respect and kindness. And to hold all parents trying to do the best by their kids with love. There is not only one way (my way/your way/our way) to raise a beautiful human.

Which seems to best sum up the problem of how to approach the gender discussion.

How often have you heard people around you express irritation and contempt about the new uses of the pronouns they/them? But why be so offended, I always ask. 'It's ridiculous/pathetic/idiotic,' the person will answer. '"They" has a meaning already. "They" means plural of "he" or "she". Why do we need to unlearn a word and change its meaning?' seems to be the nub of the objection. Language, of course, is constantly evolving. 'Apple' meant 'fruit' once upon a time, and now it means 'extremely expensive device'. 'Fruit' once meant something discriminatory, and now, in polite conversation, it does not. And so on. Few of us, if we are reasonable human beings, struggle to learn to use these words in their new forms or discard them in their old, offensive and hurtful ones.

So, why the pushback on 'they' and 'them?' I'd hate to think that the intolerance stems from distaste for a tiny, vulnerable community expressing their own needs and preferences. Why would using a pronoun requested by someone who is marginalised and vulnerable to help to make their life easier, even in the smallest way, inconvenience you at all? Listening to, acknowledging and affirming others are easy but meaningful ways to change what we do to make someone else's life better. It's not hard. It doesn't take one single thing away from you. And 'I won't be told what to say by someone else' isn't a good enough answer.

Why raising a transgender or non-binary child might be one of the hardest challenges

Vanessa says

Do all of us raise our children to a blueprint? Do we all want to raise conforming little clones of ourselves and the families around us? I'd like to think not, but regarding our children's paths, life choices and behaviour, us humans do sometimes seem to bear a strong similarity to animals in the veld.

We see security and safety in the conformity of the herd. As parents, whether we are conscious of it or not, just like mama zebra, we fear our children being different, isolated and marginalised. A lot. To a nervous parent, different could mean vulnerable and weak, zebra behaviour – that is, I think, a deeply ingrained survival strategy.

For the average person, the simplest route to safety and success, we believe, generally comes from being the best of the average, rather than a unique and entirely different version of everyone else. And many of the paths taken by our kids today may seem, to us, to be very different indeed. As parents, the closer our children are to obediently reproducing our choices, lifestyles and identities, the safer and more successful we feel.

We pride ourselves on passing on values that have served us well. Raising a child who is 'other' can rock our foundations and certainties.

Watching a child make choices that are foreign to us can result in fear: 'Will my child be happy?' 'Will they be accepted?' 'Will they succeed?' And fear, we know, can lead quickly to anger and intolerance.

I often find myself advising Villagers to parent with patience and faith in a child's eventual ability to become the *success* they want to be. What they need from us is love, optimism, understanding and support. Some thoughts:

- Our children's world is different from ours. What is strange to us is normal to them, accepted by enough of them for them to find community on whichever paths they take. A parent does not need to fear isolation and rejection on behalf of a child who appears different.
- Life is a bumpy and imperfect road. Making huge choices when we are young can affect our future health and happiness negatively – but it can also change things for the better.
- Sometimes there is no easy or right answer, no answer that will make you, as a parent, happy. But these decisions are not about you. It's your child's body, their life, their choices. Enforcing control over someone, intolerance, and lack of empathy and understanding always ends badly.
- The most important role any parent plays in their child's life is that of the loving, understanding, supportive cheerleader. Bear that in mind when you hold their most precious dreams, fears and feelings in your hands. The damage you can do by rejecting your child is more than equal to any damage hormones, surgery or the world outside can do to them.
- Get advice from experts, read widely, inform yourself. Do not confine your discussions to people you know will agree with

your starting position. Decisions made from ignorance are seldom the best decisions. And an open mind is one of a parent's most powerful tools.

- *I understand. It's so hard to see our children take paths we believe are profoundly wrong. I know a parent's pain, the fear and the wish for things to be different. Get professional support and help for yourself. It's as important that you are supported through stormy waters as it is for your child.*

Chapter 9
'LET'S TALK ABOUT MONEY, HONEY'

Skimming The Village on any given day, you get the feeling that the topic of sex is no longer a taboo. People talk to their partners, their children and their friends – and even to The Village (oh, hi, Fiery Fiona!) – about it fairly easily.

Are people this open about money? Nope.

Things have been tough lately ...

Which is not to say people aren't open with their hearts and their purses. It's amazing the levels of kindness between complete strangers on The Village. Very often the kindness has literally meant spending money from their own budgets, where we've seen people offer to buy someone electricity or send them a bag of groceries via one of the grocery apps for parents who are on the brink of disaster.

Talking frankly about the nitty-gritty of money seems harder, though.

Posts by parents at the ends of their financial tethers are almost always anonymous. When people do mention their money woes in posts that are on other topics, the issue is slid in sideways: people in difficult situations who need referrals for health or educational support, or talking about someone in their family who is depressed or anxious, will often add in something along the lines of 'financially, things have been tough lately'.

Why not talk about money?

When someone asked Villagers whether they should share information about their long-term savings with their teenagers, many people said 'No' and 'None of their beeswax'.

Joy-Anne Bromilow asked: 'Genuine question: why are people uncomfortable sharing what they earn? I don't see the need to go around telling these things to any- and everyone, but among family, friends even, why are these topics so hush-hush? Like where does this attitude stem from? I've always wondered. Not that one should burden young children with your detailed finances either way.'

Is it shame?

A lot of not wanting to talk about money to other people has to do with it not being a 'polite' topic, but in South Africa, maybe more than in any other country, it also has to do with shame of either having too little or too much. Comparison is inevitable when the differences are so stark.

Wealth versus value

Our value as human beings is not tied to how thin we are or how much extra money we have left over after the bills have been paid. We know this with our heads, but somehow, because of our training in society, we still think that people who are thin and can afford a family holiday must inherently be somehow better.

We probably need to talk about it more, though, because if money remains a taboo, it's easy to keep an unfair society going as it is, instead of questioning unfairness. The secrecy surrounding pay in companies is a lens through which to see this operate. When companies are forced to be open about salaries, the glaring inequalities are unignorable.

That's just a microcosm of the world. If all the low earners were to know what the high earners were really taking home each month, there would be mayhem.

Financial abuse

The inequalities in pay and the concerted effort to keep things quiet make it a form of abuse. It's the same in marriages and families. Money, we know, equals power, and whoever holds the purse strings call the shots.

This power situation, while it may seem benign in a partnership where one person earns the most money while the other runs the kids up and down to their activities and fetches supper on the way home, has come back to bite many a desperate Villager on the bum when the one with the moolah decides to fly the nest along with the children.

Openness about money can reduce the chances for abuse, can save families from ruin, and can preserve and build on intergenerational wealth.

Villager **Saul Smith** is a financial adviser. We asked him some questions:
Why is talking about money such a taboo?
I think with greater financial education and financial literacy, money becomes less of a taboo subject. People appear to believe that wealth equals value and this makes them fearful of being 'worth less' than the next person. For many generations people were raised with the belief that finances are a private matter and should be kept to oneself or within the confines of one's family.
Should we be more open about money in our families?
We absolutely should be more open and transparent with our families. This will lead to greater responsibility and a shared understanding of the actual financial situation. It will lead to greater clarity around expectations, and hopefully a greater level of financial literacy.

How should we talk to children about money (whether we have a lot or a little – is it different?)

Just having open communication with children is a positive. With every age and stage, it is important to impart ideas about the value of money, how it is earned, and how to use it responsibly.

When things start going badly financially and we can no longer afford first treats, and then things we always thought we could afford, do we just tell our kids? Or is that burdening them unnecessarily? Is it better to suffer in silence?

It is almost always best to be open and honest about one's financial situation. In my experience, the kids feel it when circumstances change dramatically. This can prove to be more damaging than getting the truth directly from their parents.

What is 'too much information' when it comes to talking about money?

There really isn't too much information. I would be more worried about 'too little information'. The sooner we educate ourselves and those nearest and dearest to us, the better. More often than not, families are torn apart by too little financial information. Money should be seen to walk next to us, not behind or in front. That way we can get to understand it better.

South African writer Sam Beckbessinger has become well-known for having written books about managing your money. She's also written one for teenagers, which is highly recommended. In an interview, she was asked how and when parents should start discussing money with their children. Her response was that money wasn't just about rands and cents, but about choices, and that children learn by watching.

'It's important to model good decision-making and delayed gratification for your child from the very beginning. Research shows that kids can understand basic economic ideals like value and exchange from as young as three! No matter how old your child is, there are age-appropriate ways you can start to teach them good habits.'

She also said that talking about money gets easier with practice. 'Shame doesn't help anybody, and your net worth doesn't determine your worth.'

Karin says ✓

Financial education? Ha! Nothing. Nada. Not at school. Not at home. Not at university.

My family's money culture was 'work hard and be frugal'. These are generally good values, but they are not a financial education. For years, I fumbled along in ignorance without any planning, working my butt off, but never seeing the bigger picture. The joys of compound interest, the discipline of budgeting and the smug satisfaction of having a savings goal and watching yourself inch towards it were lost on me.

Then I got divorced.

The kids still went to good schools because their father paid for that, but at home, things were tougher than anyone knew – as in 'not enough food' tough when clients paid late. There was sometimes friction around things: why couldn't they get X, Y and Z that so-and-so had? Why couldn't we just sometimes get takeaways?

So, I decided to just let them in on the whole shebang. They were six and nine at the time. I showed them how my earnings were low and erratic because of my kind of work and the fact that I am a freelancer. I laid out our expenses in full detail. I consulted them about where we could make sacrifices and what special treats we could incorporate. They learned that 'treats' did not have to cost money. They didn't know that electricity and water had to be paid for. Or Wi-Fi. They didn't know why I freaked out when they asked me to buy an avo as a special treat and then didn't eat it.

Slowly, through talking and talking and talking about money, we didn't just eliminate the friction, address the shame (of not having what their friends had) and learn to count our blessings. My children also became empowered, our domestic budget was a thing we bonded over, and they learnt life skills I know their friends didn't learn.

I have been with the same financial planners for almost two decades and they have helped me through the toughest times. They offer a free consultation for children of clients once they turn 18. I sent both my kids there the minute they were eligible. Both have had savings that come off automatically from their earnings since they started earning money every month. Expenses and savings are sorted before they plan any fun into their budgets.

They are thoughtful, frugal, and goal-orientated when it comes to money. And so much more educated about it than I was at twice their age.

Shame and anxiety about money are both still very real for me, but I had to nut up in ways I'm now glad about. My kids will no doubt have inherited some of my shame and anxiety, but at least they know how to budget.

And they have savings. Savings will save you.

Topics I covered with my kids:
- Borrowing things and returning them in good order
- Valuing and caring for what we have so we don't have to spend money unnecessarily
- Earnings versus expenses – what comes in and what goes out
- Budgeting (not 'we don't have money' but 'it's not in the budget' – if they know what's in the budget, they're more likely to understand when we can't afford something)
- Why casual debt makes you poorer and is not an option
- Delayed gratification and planning for the future
- Savings (short- and long-term)
- Interest and compound interest

- *Estate planning. This is scary for kids because of the possibility of your death, but it's also reassuring because they know you have their backs whatever life throws at them*
- *Talk about sharing, responsibility, giving, giving too much.*

What's the deal with pocket money?

People have very different attitudes towards pocket money, but there are some principles that can be incorporated or used as guidelines, as the following Village discussion showed.

Francis Slabber Günther wrote: 'Morning All. We've never given my daughter pocket money. She had started a little slime business when she was 7 which became a bigger slime business that I ran as we started doing slime parties. She had ample opportunity to work at markets and earn a commission so pocket money was earned. Lockdown resulted in us not doing any more markets and even though the slime parties continue, she can't earn pocket money from the slime sales anymore.

She's 11 now and we need to decide if we should give her some pocket money but I don't know where to start. It seems some of her friends get R200 per week (insane) and others get R10 per week (pointless). Where do we start and how do we establish a number?'

These were among the replies:

'My grandchildren get chore money. There is a chore chart on fridge and they earn money that way. R200 p.w. is OTT.' – **Dianne Robin Newcombe**

'This depends totally on what the parents expect their kids to pay for – if you expect your teen to pay for their own airtime, clothes, gifts and toiletries – R200 pw is not insane – as long as, I feel, they contribute with chores and helping ... every family is different.' – **Debbie Hawtrey**

'My daughter is 11 and she gets R300 for the month. This is her money to spend on toys etc. Chores you don't get paid for in our house, you are expected to do them to contribute as you live here as well. We explained that when u r big u earn a salary and have to budget.

So her R300 she has to budget. Sometimes she saves for 3 or 4 months and buys a big expensive Lego set. Sometimes its smaller goodies. It all goes into her own bank account linked to my hubby's who keeps check of it. Usually when they don't see the cash they don't spend it as quickly.' – Cindi Young

'A system of pocket money is R10 x their age.' – Glynne Rosselli

'I pay my son's according to their age, eg: 15 years old – R150 per month. I buy everything else that he needs, so the pocket money is either to spend at the tuckshop, or to save for the x-box games. If he has a specific item that he is wanting to buy, he then gets paid to do things around the house.' – Marlene Bowker

'R20 to R50.' – Lisa Bright

'My kids get R150 per month.' – Amy Maddams

'Are you being her UIF? ☺ I love that she was earning her own money. She sounds wonderful. I've never believed in pocket money though so I have no real input here. I believe in working for money. Chores are expected but there are options for paid jobs, e.g. washing the car or sanding the woodwork frames. Other than that birthdays and Christmas are extremely profitable ☺ but free money is not a lesson I want to teach my kids.' – Yvette Morris

'Maybe I'm alone here but I don't believe in pocket money. What do they need to pay for? They are fed, clothed, have toys, possibly phones etc. Chores are a responsibility they need to learn as they are part of the family and everyone needs to contribute. It also teaches them to do things for themselves and for others without outside motivation like pocket money. I like the business idea because that teaches her that she needs to work for her money but like Yvette said the idea of "free" money is not a lesson I want my kids to learn either … ☺' – Leeat Confait

'Teach her the magic of compound interest. If she starts now little by little and never withdrawing from that account she will be astounded by the amount when she is twenty!' – Careena Bernstein

Household chores are a given with no extra payment, even chores that go above and beyond. I don't believe in monetary reward for kindness or helping. Pocket money is a privilege and not a salary.' – **Robyn Clark Bosch**

'My boys are 12 and 15, don't really need anything so R10 x age … not much, but all I have to give …!' – **Pamela Nienaber**

'I read somewhere once the formula is age x days in the month. Eg 10 year old will get R300 per month.' – **Marlize Lombard Du Toit**

What to do when things get tough?

An anonymous poster was considering suicide because she'd lost her job. She was a single parent and she didn't know what to do next.

Jo-ann Stokes replied: 'My dad was great with money (he was an average earner, but knew how save) but his advice to me when I was a young mom and we were battling, if you cannot put bread on the table, then don't do insurances. You have to worry first and foremost about today, not tomorrow, until you are back on your feet. Be honest with your son, they aren't stupid and if I have to be honest, kids whose parents battle and don't have everything given to them on a platter usually do better in adult life and are more successful. Stop what you can't afford, and rather be there for your son … he would rather have you with him than the material things in life. You are more important to him than playing sports or going to a private school.'

And **Karen Balt** wrote: 'As an only child raised by a single mother, she sat me down at 12 years old and made me aware of the lack of finances and from then onward it became a team effort for us to survive with suggestions and options discussed and implemented as we went along, so I agree, talk to your son and hopefully he will have some ideas that will help. Make it your one year project together.'

Solid moves in slippery times

The past few years have been a harrowing time financially for South Africa. The extent of the problem – especially since the COVID years – is clear from the many posts from desperate parents.

Some have already had to walk the path of tightening belts and reassessing finances, and they have had some wonderful advice. We skimmed The Village for some of the most basic, useful and helpful money tips:

- Finances are an ongoing negotiation because nothing stays the same. Regular reviewing must be built into your year.
- Make a budget. Stick to it.
- Don't lend something – including money – unless you can live with not getting it back.
- Make use of National Wills Week (usually in September) to make sure that your will is in order.
- Every now and again, write down every single cent you spend for a month. You can identify money leaks that way and reassess your spending.
- Pay yourself before you do anything else. That means a percentage of your salary must automatically be paid into a savings account before you pay anything else. Villagers recommend a 32-day notice account, because you can't simply withdraw on a whim.
- Don't buy for the sake of buying or boredom or some other non-reason. Responsible consumerism saves money *and* saves the planet.
- Stay busy. If you stay busy, you don't have time to wander around the shops buying stuff or spend time online popping things into the basket icon.
- Many Villagers recommend a Facebook group called 1Family-1Stockpile for tips to get your finances running smoothly.
- Use the app 22Seven to budget. **Stephanie Altendorfer Moore** wrote: 'I literally have a full overview of my entire financial

portfolio, spending, value of every asset up-to-date from month to month. I love this budgeting tool because it categorises all my spending and cuts out the admin for me. It's absolutely brilliant.'
- Another app that makes sense is Splitwise if you have to share payments for things. It works very well for holiday planning and for big family celebrations where everyone is contributing.
- Don't make debt. If you have debt, make paying it off your number one priority. Debt is very expensive.
- Address shopping addictions. Get to the root cause and work on eliminating it before it cripples you.
- **Pumza Mweli** had this idea for if you need cash but have forgotten your purse at home: go into your banking app and send the money to yourself and then withdraw at an ATM.
- Get into thrift shopping. Get into factory shopping. Get into clothes swap events.

On grocery buying and family meals

- Don't take the kids shopping. **Vicki Sleet** says: 'Taking them to the shops is like warfare!'
- But then **Charles Nolte Marais** has a take on this too. He agreed that it was warfare, but 'when it comes to check out and pushing the trolley to the car and packing it in, you really wish they were with you'. His compromise is to allow them to choose four items each once a month.
- Eat less meat. Become vegetarian. Focus on plant foods and stay away from processed foods, which are more expensive and less healthy anyway.
- Raw vegetable meals (i.e. salads) also save on electricity costs.
- Eliminate food waste. This takes thought, effort and planning. Your environmentally concerned children will be proud of your consciousness. Rope them into this mission to make them feel

- like they're doing something useful for the planet, while you save money.
- Meal planning is crucial for saving money. Also, for saving time, effort and the environment.
- Shop online. **Georgina Guedes** says she has reduced her bills radically without even trying 'just because of no impulse buying'.
- Go to the shops after 4 p.m. to find fresh things whose prices have been reduced at the end of the day. Do it on the way home from work to save petrol.
- Packed lunches for everyone: school, work and outings too. Imagine both adults spending R50 a day on food or coffees away from home. That's R100 a day times about 20 working days a month. That's R2 000 a month you could be putting into a holiday fund.
- Eat with the seasons.
- Buy local.
- Neighbourhood Facebook groups often have people offering surplus from their gardens or kitchen for free or at very low prices.
- Grow as much of your own food as you can, even if it's just a pot of rosemary and parsley.

Financial independence

South Africa's Domestic Violence Act (and its more recent amendment) recognises economic exploitation as a form of domestic abuse. People who try to control their partners' ability to make a living, or force them to relinquish control of their assets or income or management of finances, are abusers.

Linda Lion wrote: 'Regular conversations about money, fairness, energy input, gratitude and generosity remain essential [in happy partnerships].'

One Villager, speaking from experience, has some advice to offer from her position as someone who was exploited financially by a partner:

'I am seeing way too many posts about women stuck in toxic relationships because they do not have the finances to leave.

'I left my first marriage with nothing but my clothes and my five-month old. I still don't know how we survived.

'Four years later, I left a narcissist who emotionally abused me and tried to use finances to control me, but I'd already learnt the hard lessons and put myself back together better than before.

'Here's some life advice for women (everyone actually) that made my [second] escape that much less scary and uncertain than the first:

1. Always have you own income or means to earn an income.
2. Don't let your partner know what you earn unless they absolutely have to.
3. Have an emergency fund or saving account and pray you never have to use it.
4. [Have a] Driver's license even if you don't own a car (yet).
5. Don't put anything in their name that you pay for.
6. Children: courts consider the well-being of a child and not the luxury of life each parent could offer. Money doesn't determine guardianship. Not unless they caught you with 50kg of heroin standing over a dead body with a smoking gun and 15 witnesses will you lose your child.
7. [Be wary of] Pie crust promises: easily made easily broken.

'Before making financial decisions in the passion of the moment image an instance where you absolutely hate each other and are out for the kill: what smart decision can you make now to protect yourself when it's not all sunshine and roses?

'Abusers take advantage of people who are dependent on them. Always maintain your independence.

'I am happily married to a wonderful man now and I thank my stars each day for him. But I still have followed each of the above to the letter.

'Plan for the worst and hope for the best because the worst always finds people who deserve it the least.'

What happens if you die?

It's not a question we or our children like to contemplate, but not planning for death can leave your children completely at sea in the unlikely event that it happens.

Lesley Scott noted that we are all reminded to make sure we have measures in place to take care of our minor children in the event of our death, 'but what about our kids over 18?' she asked in The Village. What do your young adult children know about your estate planning, where your documents are kept, who to contact if you pass away, what your end-of-life choices are?

'I have heard of two recent instances where young adults were orphaned as a result of Covid. In the one case, all other family is overseas and in the other, only a very elderly and infirm older relative remains. These youngsters are now in a position of having to make decisions, arrange funerals, deal with all the formalities of death, while mourning and worrying about their own futures.

'How do you think we should prepare our young adult (possibly still dependent or partially dependent) kids for this scenario?'

Vanja Karth contributed: 'My 12-year-old knows which drawer all my death paperwork is in. I have written a cover letter with details of what work insurance covers, what bank insurance covers, what other life/funeral/death covers there is … etc. being a single mom I have a very comprehensive plan and will around my son's care. And best friend up the road knows where all the paperwork is too.'

Bridget Eddy said her daughter knows exactly how to gain access to everything. 'I've told her a million times and have a checklist of things for her. My will is incredibly detailed to ensure everything is taken care of.'

Liz Moran's advice is to get your wills and powers of attorney in order. 'Even if you feel like you'll live forever, it is a nightmare for those left behind. If you love your spouse, partner, children, parents, etc. there's even more reason to get your docs in order. You may be young, but you can't predict what's around the corner.'

Many people advise an estate planning file or document that contains all the necessary information in one place. It should list medical and medical aid information; bank, policy, insurance and investment account details; subscription, licence and membership lists (and renewal dates); and online and social media info and passwords. It can also contain a list of wishes about how to distribute personal possessions. It's vital to have a will and to have appointed an executor who you know will be fair, efficient and trustworthy when it comes to handling your estate.

Vanessa says

In another of our chapters, we look at the very best advice one can give another parent. All of it could be, I think, distilled into one sentence: 'You are enough.'

This is really important to remember when you are considering (perhaps bemoaning) the connection between successful parenting and money. On your dark days, do you secretly believe you would be a better parent if you had more money? Luckily, for the vast majority of us, money is not *what is most needed if our aim is to be beloved parents.*

Years ago, I worked with Oprah Winfrey. We published O, The Oprah Magazine *in South Africa for ten wonderful years. To launch it, we did masses of research, trying to get to grips with the needs, passions and beliefs of our potential audience. We asked one question that, at the time, I pooh-poohed, thinking that, of course, everyone would answer 'Madiba' and we'd learn nothing.*

*The question was, 'Who do you respect more than anyone else?'
The answer was not Madiba.
The answer was, 'My mother.'*

How beautiful is that? In a country and a demographic where many of the mothers concerned had had to work away from their own children, work in menial, time-consuming jobs to get by, these daughters valued their moms above all. And why? Because the following does not cost a bean:

- *To be a child's cheerleader. To be the voice in their head and heart that says, 'You can do it!' 'I believe in you!' 'I'm here to try to help if you need me.' 'I love you for you.' To be the voice who says, 'You are enough.'*
- *To also be the voice that says, 'I am enough.' To parent with self-respect. To role model optimism, dignity, courage, resilience and decency.*
- *To hold your own head up high, no matter what.*
- *To try to inoculate your children against the corrupt and plastic value system of social media. Talk, talk, talk to your children. Talk to them, when they push their noses up against the virtual showroom windows, behind which gleam possessions they and you cannot afford. There are important values to be learnt through not having everything: sustainability, modesty, living within one's means, learning the true value of things …*
- *To teach a set of values that ranks being a net contributor and a decent citizen higher than being rich.*
- *To be a parent who respects everyone and treats everyone with equal respect: be the person who treats the waitron and office cleaner as decently as you treat the most successful person you know. Children are sponges. They take in much more by osmosis than they do by being told.*

When things seem bleak

Chapter 10

THE LONELY CHILD

Have you heard the comment that a mother is only ever as happy as her unhappiest child? The teen years, as we all know by now, are filled with challenges for our children, and as our offspring suffer, we do too.

Loneliness is one of these challenges. Teens are not the only demographic suffering its effects, but studies show that some age groups are more vulnerable to experiencing feelings of isolation and disconnection. According to a study by the Kaiser Family Foundation, young adults aged 18–24 report feeling lonely at higher rates than other age groups.

We may imagine that our crime statistics and economic challenges could mean that our children have a harder time socialising than their peers overseas, but *Psychology Today* (PT) reports that the British Broadcasting Corporation (BBC) recently did a large national survey and found that 4 out of 10 young people aged 16–24 were pretty lonely, describing themselves as: feeling misunderstood (not unexpected in teens); sad; suffering from FOMO (fear of missing out); not having anyone to talk with; and feeling detached from the world.

PT lists the following reasons teens suffer:
- The loss of a loved one

- Exclusion from peers, family and community
- A sense of detachment, alienation, of not belonging.

All of these have serious consequences for the mental and physical health of our children and families.

The South African condition

Happy humans, as we've said before, are meant to live in safe, thriving, bustling, dynamic, intergenerational communities. If you can, imagine an actual village square and a tree with youngsters, parents and elders gathered underneath it after a hard day's work. Children playing, adults shelling peas, youngsters flirting. In a more contemporary environment, imagine a European town square, with bars and restaurants filled with people, enjoying themselves, socialising and connecting.

In South Africa, we retreat to our homes behind bars. We watch over our children with anxiety and fear. We track their every move and clip their wings in the name of safety. Our children run the very real risk of retreating to the company of their devices, scrolling through others' social media feeds, wondering why the peers they thought were their friends are out somewhere without them – or to a dark cave and the addictive and engrossing company of their game consoles.

The social landscape of tweens and teens is also not a simple place. One day a child can be 'in'; the next, banished, cancelled or just dropped. Few children are going to be happy if they're home alone on a Saturday afternoon when everyone else is at the beach or at the Queen Bee's house. Friend groups are fragile, unstable entities, with even popular kids engaged in a scramble for loyalty and security. And bullying is sadly not uncommon among all groups of kids. I used to think that girls used their fangs and claws and boys used their fists, but in the end it doesn't really matter which weapons are deployed.

Ground Zero of teenage need comes at a time when our children slam the door on us and appear to need their friends much more than they need us.

How do we help?

Here are some tips for supporting a child through a lonely period:

- **Keep them busy.** Invest in every sport or hobby you can afford. Or just put in the hours yourself to support them. For kids who struggle with relationships with others, team sports may not be the answer – navigating team dynamics includes popularity wars that are as vicious as playground politics (goalie bullying in football, water polo and hockey is a thing!).

    Look out for activities that will suit sporty but lonely children. Horses are therapeutic. So are surfing, skateboarding, ice-skating; anything immersive that takes up time and introduces them to new peer groups will do.

    For the nerdy kids ('nerdy' is a compliment these days, btw): chess. Start by introducing them to Chess.com, then chess club, then real-life tournaments. I asked parents on The Village whether anyone had a kid who wanted to coach my youngest in chess. Result: he found one of his most beloved pals that way!

- **Enforce family time** so hours are eaten up: Sundays are for family hikes, outings etc. Climbing mountains with their parents is not most teenagers' first-prize activity for an endless summer, but mine remember those walking, exploring weekends fondly. The trick is to announce the event on Wednesday: 'You can't do anything on Sunday – we are having a family day.' It takes the pressure off.

- **Pull in the aunties and the uncles** whether they're blood relations or not (you can always ask friends to help). There is no shame in needing other adults to reach back to your child. Do the same for theirs.

- **Encourage volunteering.** Get your child or older teen to walk rescue dogs, read to the elderly, join any charitable organisation, join the Scouts, take up lifesaving. The skills learnt in these organisations, the friends made, the benefit to a youngster's health – both mental and physical – are all invaluable, and they eat up time on weekends.
- **Get them earning.** Babysitting, tutoring, dog-walking for cash. These activities take up time when other peers may be socialising. Earning money can offset the loss of 'fun' and commitments offset the 'shame' of being alone.
- **Board games:** Board game geeks meet in cafés and welcome all comers. The games are immersive and transporting. And they take hours. Honestly, board games are brilliant – and underrated.
- **Don't shame them by being negative about their online gaming.** For someone who is lonely, the console and the friends made through it can be a lifesaver – the only trick is to ensure that online gaming is not *all* the kid is doing.

Everyone will be lonely at some point. Do not fear it for your child or panic when there seems to be no end to it. You can teach many good lessons to a child who is not swept up in the social whirl: self-sufficiency, optimism, the understanding that hard days come and go, the value of parents and the 'uncool'. Accept that, if you have a lonely child, the responsibility for mainlining attention, love, fun and company in the absence of buddies will probably be up to you. My husband always said, 'It's better if the kids are unhappy and alone out of home and loved and safe *at* home than the other way around'.

In 2023, the wonderful writer Kate Mosse said on the iconic BBC radio programme *Desert Island Discs* that the reason she was always confident, courageous and ready to take risks was because she had always been safe and loved at home. You cannot underestimate the importance of one solid, loving rock (aka you).

As Villager **Andrea Tocknell** wrote: 'The bitchiness and brat-pack mentality of preteens and teens is brutal! My girls both chose to swim against the current, chose quality friends, not quantity, didn't care about being excluded because they KNEW that they had a parent who was fully invested and taught them how to value themselves.

'Both had a hell of a confusing, lonely, mixed experience at school, but chose to stick it out. Character building!

'Now, gentle, compassionate but feisty young ladies. They "grew a pair" through adversity and look back in gratitude for the life lessons.

'Love your [child] through this. Teach them that to fit in with bitchy frenemies makes them part of a pack, but not special. Standing apart, keeping your integrity even at the expense of your popularity, is wayyyyy more valuable.'

Words to share with your lonely child

Author Brianna Wiest gives excellent advice that could help. She urges us not to hold on to the people who aren't ready to love us. Letting go of these people is incredibly hard, she says, but crucial. We need to stop trying to be accepted by the people around us who have no desire to change, and to acknowledge that 'You're not for everyone and not everyone is for you'. Instead of changing who we are, she says, we should strive for a life of 'joy, interest and commitment', and see who is ready to follow us into that life.

It's important, she believes, to recognise the difference between love and attachment. Our bonds to those who are attached to us could simply fade away if we stop investing our energy to maintain them. But love is different – and it's not our job to save people or be responsible for them. Letting go of harmful people frees up the time and energy we'd be better off spending on loving relationships with 'healthy, prosperous people'. Only then will we gain 'love, esteem, happiness and protection' – all of which we deserve.

More thoughts from The Village

Admin **Kim Penstone** also encourages out-of-school activities: 'School is often the place where kids are loneliest, so finding something within the school environment often doesn't help. Things to do outside of school, friends from different social spheres and of different ages can help to balance the scales a bit.'

'I think it's really important to teach kids (and adults) the difference between being lonely and being alone,' wrote **Lesley Scott**, also one of The Village admins. 'I would also say that we have all forgotten how to be bored. Boredom can make you feel lonely if you don't know how to just "be".

'Also teach them about the difference between superficial and deeper connections. You can be lonely in a room full of people, or perfectly content on your own.

'As a parent, do not automatically assume that a child or teen that is not social is lonely. Also remember that teens especially often have active online social lives – even if they are not socialising in person.

'If your child expresses that they are lonely, try to determine why. Are they feeling excluded, do they not know how to engage with strangers, do they feel they are different to their peers? If you understand the problem, you can begin looking for a solution.

'For introverts, interacting socially with others can be stressful and exhausting. Things like gaming, board games, chess, hint hunts or escape rooms allow for interaction without too much expectation from others of things like conversation, eye contact etc. Sporty introverts might prefer individual sports like tennis, golf, cycling etc. where people are around but not too much interaction is needed.

'Extroverts are more likely to feel lonely if they can't top up their tanks with social interaction. Team sports, volunteering, dancing, drama as well as activities like gaming and board games are all good.

'And no matter who you are: books, books, books. If you are feeling lonely in this world, you can immerse yourself in the world of your book. For many people, reading is a literal life saver.'

Zann Hoad agrees with Lesley: 'Get kids excited about reading. You're never lonely with a good book. The trick is to keep trying books until they find one that floats their boat. No one wants to read a book that they find boring or is too challenging. Libraries are great for books. It's practically free!'

Find the good guys and draw them in

'One step at a time. You need to help. Invite someone over for an hour or two. Then ask another to join you on a picnic etc. etc. Eventually it will come, the friendships,' said **Katrien Dehaeck**. 'I worked hard at it too and it paid off. Good luck. Don't despair. Also, they do not need a lot of friends. One or two good ones will do.'

Caroline Gelderblom agrees: 'There are tools which can help but yes you could actively support the younger tweens by organising one-on-one play dates. [At school] perhaps they could get involved with helping with the younger grades or in the library. Read a book in those quiet moments. You could build up plans for how a lonely or excluded child could deal with these experiences in advance. But understanding what makes your child tick will help them find their tribes. Children on the spectrum are often targeted by bullies. They might be socially awkward and get on better with adults. I advise parents to get a child who is repeatedly excluded assessed. For those who are neurodiverse high school is often better, especially if you prepare them well.'

'By the time you realise, often the damage is done. So a parent's role often is to support the recovery,' noted **Georgia Argyropoulos**. 'It's important to boost social skills and confidence by teaching coping strategies for confidence anxiety and conversational skills for tricky moments. Good luck. I've been there. As a child, even as an adult. Best encourage the search for a small group of good humans. Then watch our children flourish.'

'I straighten her little tiara every morning – I lift her chin and remind her that she is meant for greater things than playground bullies,' writes **Dohne Green**. 'I remind her about all her good qualities, her kindness, her love for animals and to remember that good friends will take the time and care for her and the ones who don't, are not her friends and that's ok as well. I encourage her to speak up when she's hurt and to not be a push over but to also accept that she isn't going to be everyone's cup of tea.

'I have also identified the one or two friends that are good for her and arranged play dates – these are a great success! And I have engaged the school counselor to be proactive about the girl group dynamics and to give her the safe space if she needs it.

'I've taught her to check in with herself when feeling reactive and overwhelmed and to remove herself so as not to make things worse. The only place we have control is how we react – teaching her about her boundaries and to seek out positive opportunities is very empowering.'

Introverts may be perfectly happy not seeing schoolmates outside of school

Fiona Pfeiffer says that her 14-year-old son has friends at school but doesn't see them outside school. 'He is passionate about rock climbing so we have joined a group and do lots of climbing with the group members. They are all adults but he is so happy to interact with like-minded people, no matter the age.

'It's hard for me as I don't climb but I take a book and relish a bit of me time whilst he has happy time. Getting him out is important as he is just glued to YouTube at home so we also go on lots of walks and bike rides. I am also not a "groupie" so I understand where he comes from. Try and find a hobby/sport as long as he is happy.'

Kirsty Galliard has a similar story to tell: 'My son is a superintrovert and not that interested in hanging out with his mates outside of school or sports as he is a science nerd, and most teenage boys are more interested in girls and parties (according to him). I suggested a regular game of Padel with a few friends, and he loved it. The best thing about Padel is that even the most unsporty person (me!) can enjoy it. Most Padel social clubs have a restaurant where you can order some pizzas and drinks afterwards. That and mountain biking with his dad or playing touch rugby in a social league have been game-changers!

'He also entered the Eskom Expo for Young Scientists and made it to the national round where he met many, lovely, like-minded science types, some of whom are also interested in mountain biking and trail running. Being at a boys school, he also met some nice girls with shared interests.'

'I have found that activities outside of school have been the best as it is a safe space where they can tap into their talents and meet like minded friends,' says **Kilona Radia**. 'Keep these varied in the early years. Know when their social batteries are being depleted, as alone may be a happy place for a while. Chess was a big one for us. Rubix cubing is another great one and there is a whole speed-cubing community out there that I never knew existed!

'Tapping into their entrepreneurial spirit is another, coupled with whatever they love doing, whether it's arts and craft, baking, doing a training session on Roblox or Minecraft for newbies. Right now we are working on making candles for a piggy bank market and we have gone through learning about Excel and budgeting – all while being alone at home. Love Lesley's comment on the difference between lonely and alone. Sometimes alone is when the brain processes who we really are and what we really love doing.'

A few more ideas

'Rowing and golf are also good sports options if team sports don't work. Drama class and art class have been great for us.' – **Bryony van Wyk**

'I was pleased my husband got my boys into fishing. Great for holidays at the sea and then they got into competitive fly fishing and loved it. Quite an expensive hobby though. Good to destress – out for the day in nature.' – **Janet Labberte**

'Involve lonely children in a charity with other kids to help the community so they meet people their own age. Community is a great place for confidence to be restored.' – **Michelle Levy Kaplan**

If your child is not lonely ...

Chantal Malan has this advice: 'Teach your kid to look out for the neurodivergent, shy or queer kid. They don't need to befriend them, just be kind and don't bully them. They already feel lonely and misunderstood. You and your child's opinion about their disability or sexual identity and orientation shouldn't be the last thing they hear before they decide to end it all. If you can't be inclusive, please don't be cruel.'

This comforting and hopeful post was loaded in 2020 by a Villager who requested to be anonymous:

'I want to share a word from the other side, with the parents of children who struggle. Who walk stormy, messy, snotty, gritty, grotty, teary, rocky paths through adolescence. Whose children are the ones who are lonely, maybe sad and/or always in trouble at school. Who sit alone at lunch break, while all the others easily jostle, banter, laugh and tease and post their happiness where those without can't but see, their noses pressed up against the window of social media.

'A word to parents whose kids aren't even happily bumping along with "average".

'We had one of those. A high school "999 what's your emergency?" Haha bitter laugh. Choose a card, any card. We've drawn the full deck. Just not the King or Queen. Maybe a pack filled with jokers. But this pity party isn't fun or funny. Is it?

'Well, maybe if black humour is your jam. "Where's my head girl?" I scream silently to myself, waiting in the headmaster's office for the

15th time. "Maybe this isn't the school for you, my dear. Have you thought perhaps about other options?" Where's my kid, who was just supposed to be just like everyone else's kid? That would do. I'm not asking for too much, am I? Just like everyone else's kid would do.

'Why am I mopping up tears on Sunday afternoons; why am I not watching her and her lovely friends (fragments of my fantasies) laughing in the den and around the pool that we built for our dreams of her popular teenage years?

'Why am I gifted panic attacks, fallouts from friend after friend, disciplinary hearings? A dark smelly bedroom. Cigarettes. Piercings. Tattoos! Changes of schools, home schools, no school, lonely endless weekends, staring at each other, me and him, wondering what to say to her. Out of excuses. Can't say "It's not you, it's them" ONE MORE TIME. "But we love you" isn't enough.

'More tears. Many nights, both of us, she and me, tossing and turning, spooning, in her single bed. To comfort both of us, let me be honest here. It wasn't only her in pain. Spooning while her schoolmates were at the sleepovers she wasn't invited to.

'Parental stomach churning. Smiling tightly at the Grade PTA awkwardly moving away from the parents of the children who've rejected mine.

'Our path.

'And now we've walked out of it. She's 26. Those painful days are far behind us.

'I suppose you think I'm going to say it's all ok, hallelujah! she left school, found her people and it all miraculously "came right", just like that?

'No. Life doesn't seem to work that way. What happened instead was that she grew in strength. She became accustomed to the pain that life provides as lessons, if you choose to accept them. She's benefited from doing the work that those years in therapy demanded. She became better at finding her own particular joy, without waiting for others to provide. She's less bothered by the slings and arrows of adult reality that I notice every now and then seem to pierce her peers. She's ok. She's good at holding her pain.

'She's learned to sift through her landscape (still sometimes a bit harsh) to find the gems buried there. One good friend. Or two. A loving boyfriend. A passion for beauty she can enjoy alone. (We thank the lord for classical music – so transporting, so healing.) We acknowledge her robustness, her resilience and her strength. Her ability to arm herself against the bad days, and yet still glow with gratitude and joy when things do go her way. None of that to be taken for granted.

'A greater empathy for others in pain than she would have had, had she danced through her teenage years. That's what teenage years are there for, I realise – just too late for my grey hair and wrinkles. Today she's a teacher. A wonderful teacher. She's the teacher who sits quietly next to the kicking, screaming, sulking, trouble-making adolescent, behind the bike shed and says, "I get it. I'm here if you need me."

'We couldn't be prouder.'

Chapter 11

DANGER AND DISASTER

If there is a limit to the number of things we should worry about when it comes to our teenagers' safety, can someone please show us where it is? So that we can run through every worst-case scenario, freak right the hell out, and enter a new phase of divine acceptance that we have little control about where and when the bomb of catastrophe is likely to fall?

Danger

That parents worry about their children's safety – some parents more than others, to the point where their worry itself becomes a kind of danger for the child – is part of what happens when you become the ward of a young person. You're meant to worry. That's your job.

But in South Africa, being more worried than parents in other countries is an entirely sane response. We have a history of ingrained violence. Huge parts of the population have been terrorised by the state. Men kill each other in drunken fights or in road rage incidents. Boys rape. Men rape. Fathers murder their wives and children and then kill themselves. Homes are invaded, and people are tied up and tortured. Accidents! Fires! Floods! Teachers and preachers are molesters.

Police are untrustworthy. Systems are nonexistent, failing or corrupt.

Tamlyn Pawson asked The Village: 'I desperately need to hear what parents do to prevent debilitating anxiety taking hold.' Anxiety, she said, made her feel ineffectual.

How do we keep a handle on our own fears while trying to teach our children to be safe without freaking them out? How do you prepare them for *every* danger when there are dangers not even our darkest imaginings can conjure? How do you find joy and meaning while also staying safe?

Melanie Loebenberg Novitzkas, speaking about crime, said that her 14-year-old daughter was jumpy and watchful and pushed furniture up against the door when they went away and wanted to sleep with a knife beside her. 'I don't live in crippling fear or in denial or believe fake news,' Melanie said. 'What I see and experience is real. I am very aware of the reasons for crime. I am a social worker. I get it. I worked with neglected, abandoned and abused boys. I think my feelings mirror many other South Africans. This is my home and I love it, but I don't feel safe here. One can be hyper aware but not excessively fearful.'

As parents, we have a duty to get a handle on our own fear first and foremost. The fine balance between preparing, planning and scanning the environment on one hand, and feeling free enough to allow our children to explore the limits of their capabilities on the other, can feel impossible to maintain.

It may be our most important work, though. We want our children to be able to head out into the world with the kind of confidence and knowledge they can use when we are not around to protect them. They *have* to learn to look after themselves. And *we* have to teach them how to do that.

Emma Arogundade believes she hasn't succeeded in managing her anxiety. 'I realised too late that I was living with hardcore anxiety and that likely my mom was too and our desire to control and keep safe has manifested in a lot of "don't do that" kind of stuff. And Covid really amped up "the world is a dangerous place" narrative.'

Fear isn't all bad

Fear is natural. It is good and right for children to have some fear and some hesitancy because it means they are tuning into the environment, their bodies and their intuition. We mostly have built-in monitors for what feels safe and what doesn't. We want our kids to be a bit fearful, especially since it seems like children who seem entirely fearless also show less empathy and are more aggressive than their peers, according to a study at the University of Haifa.

Since little kids pattern their responses to the world by looking at us, we have to find a way to show a golden thread between using natural fear to help us and avoiding everything because it's all so scary.

Village parents have some great advice about managing your own issues and over-the-top responses so that your children understand how to keep themselves safe.

Shaheeda Davids Cooper, a mother of two girls, one 16 and the other 19 and with a driver's licence, says she's not sure that you get better at managing fear as your children grow, partly also because from toddler to teenager to semi-adult, your anxiety changes as your child grows. 'It's up to you to control your own anxiety and fears. Easier said than done, especially in South Africa. I find that being honest helps. It gets harder as they grow older and want more freedom. I still battle my inner demons and they often point it out to me, but I'm slowly managing my anxiety with having two daughters who want to go places and have experiences.'

Desiree Pretorius points out that parents' fear reactions are sometimes triggered by past experiences. 'If, for example, you have lost a child, or had a child with a severe illness, or watched a parent go through a trauma, then one tends to be overprotective. I think we, as parents, do the best we can with the knowledge we have and the experiences we have had. Our growth comes from acknowledging our trauma and experiences and trying to not be a helicopter parents with that knowledge. But it's extremely hard.'

Bronwen Goldby said she had two very busy young kids. She used to 'scream loudly and very high pitched inside myself A LOT!!!! I often turned away so I couldn't see when they climbed jungle gyms, etc. I kept calm on the surface. I would calmly walk them through those moments: look at where the steps are, keep focused, well done, you're doing great, hold on to the rail etc. But I wouldn't stop them unless truly I felt they were totally out of their depth ... I had to trust in their (age-appropriate) ability so they would grow confident within themselves and their bodies; confident to take appropriate risks and push boundaries.

'And I had to recognise and acknowledge what was my anxiety.

'I think a lot of parenting confident kids is quietly being in the background just outside their vision so they are not aware. You are ready to catch them if they fall, but the confidence and joy they feel when they don't fall and feel they have done it without you!'

Lisl van der Hoven suggests that imparting ways of being safe to your children without freaking them out is to start with connection. 'Connection is the key. Connection to yourself as a parent – knowing and sharing your own insecurities and vulnerabilities, and showing courage by walking through them instead of avoiding them entirely.

'Connection to your children. Sharing the wonder of life and wholeheartedly living it without being afraid all the time. Cautioning gently and having real conversations as they grow older.

'Connection to themselves. Teaching them confidence, how to trust their intuition and how to love and value themselves enough.

'Children and teenagers watch and mirror us. All. The. Time.

'A child can become immune to a mother's constant fear and anxiety. They tune out and turn off and away. The results can sometimes be disastrous.'

Mandy Warner says you need to pick your non-negotiable safety issues. 'For instance: always have car booster and seatbelts on. No opening of gate without mom or dad around. No going out of my sight in a public play area or other public places. Then, with things like monkey bars, I warned them about height, and I would be close by and let them try. Same with skateboards, bikes, roller skates.

'They need to be able to fall and learn and find things out for themselves. I find if I keep to the rules I have set myself, it gives me an element of control and helps with the anxiety.'

Seqel Hall believes in facts, not fear. 'I keep things factual and not fearful. Have done so since my son was a toddler. I never assumed he was too small to have a proper conversation or to understand.

'Just be honest with your child. They have to live in this shitty world, so we have to prepare them for it. It's our duty above all else. There's no point in concealing the truths. The world is extremely dangerous. People are dangerous and our children are responsible for their own survival as much as we are. Teach them that. Encourage questions. Encourage exploration of topics, places or things. Discourage fear.'

Tasneem Grimwood Van der Merwe, a teacher and a mother of three 'strong-willed fearless toddlers' who are now grown-up and independent, says that as a single mother, she had her work cut out for her. 'I looked ahead to the future and envisioned them leaving my cocoon to venture out into the world, without me, and it bloody terrified me. To the point that I wanted to smother them in love and "stuff" just to make them never want to leave.'

One day, as the children started school, Tasneem was hit by 'one of the most powerful waves of enlightenment'.

'My daughter walked into her new school and patted me on the shoulder and said, "It's okay Mom, you'll be fine. You have friends at school." (She was referring to my job as a teacher.) She took her brother's hand and off they went, him with tears in his eyes but waving and smiling through it.

'I then realised that if I was going to say goodbye to them in twenty years' time, I would have to start modifying my behaviour slowly, gently and surely.

'I would drop them off outside school, wave and drive off. No walk-ins, unless invited. I watched every single cricket, hockey, waterpolo match and swimming gala, screaming loudly, but at least six rows back. I never mailed teachers to question decisions. They had to do that and tackle their own problems. I stayed out of friendship issues – too fickle. I pushed them a little at a time to try new things and pretend to be excited, but I was darn terrified inside. I encouraged taking chances and risks, taught them how to fall safely with me perched out of sight around the corner.

'Fast forward 19 years. My daughter finished matric, was not ready to study, so went to London to au pair. She did two years and travelled to many countries. Alone. My son and some friends chose not to do Matric Rag and went to Bali for two weeks. He was scared. I was terrified, but I smiled and cheered, then cried while he boarded the flight. In a few months, he will be leaving for Cambodia and my heart is shattered. But he won't know that.

'Because my heart's anxiety should not be owned by them. Then next year, it will be my baby daughter's turn. Off to new adventures while Mom pretends to hold it together.

'So my advice is, start with bite-sized pieces. Give age-appropriate space, but be present for when things flop.

'Engage, encourage and always empathise. Their lived experiences are often the only ones they care about.

'And their paths will always be just that: THEIR path. Let go of their hands slowly, and one day they will be the ones to reach out for yours.'

Disaster

Terrible things – all our worst nightmares – can and do happen to parents in The Village. Arrest, drugs, addictions, false accusations, missed exams, disciplinaries, terrible rejections and devastating break-ups, failure leading to repeat of academic years, sexual assault ... you name it.

Some disasters are caused by our children. Some are caused by other children. Or by teachers. Or by complete outsiders. Or by no one in particular. So it's hard to sort our initial responses into things that make sense, as we are overwhelmed by shock, blame, anger, indignation, disbelief and every other confusing negative emotion.

This anonymous Villager's post captures some of the confusion of the moment when you become aware that things are not the way you thought they were:

'I have a daughter in Grade 8.

'She has been caught vaping, videos of it, eating and supplying dagga cookies, alcohol at school, and now suspension all in one term.

'She is a beautiful kind child, can be intimidating to peers because she is a natural sports person and loves having fun. She is a non-judgemental person and owns up to things when she makes a mess.

'There are indications that that something has happened in her past which she doesn't want to speak about. She is also cutting and writing very planned suicide notes.

'Please can I have some thoughts on punishment.'

There are so many things this parent is worrying about in this post, but her admiration and love for her daughter still glimmer through. Punishment is probably not indicated in this situation, but we carry our parenting scripts over from a generation who believed all of parenting amounted to punishment for every perceived wrongdoing. And we are seldom equipped for trouble like the kind above; we reach for what we know. Many Villagers have pointed this out: that what our children need when they act out is not necessarily punishment.

With teenagers, though, the line between cries for help and pushing boundaries is blurred. One Villager reminded other parents not to pathologise every misstep our teens make as they try to figure themselves out:

'I'm posting this anonymously because people are going to hate me for this message.

'Parents, you are not doing anything wrong if your kid rebels, but sneaks around behind your back, has underage sexual experiences, tries drugs, drinks too much alcohol, bunks school or backchats.

'Can we please just remember these kids are just that, they are kids and they will f@&k up a lot. It's their job to make mistakes and your job to clean up after them and support them.

'Don't be devastated if your kid drinks too much and you find him vomiting all over the show, he is going through real things and trying to figure out what the hell this life is all about.

'Can we not treat our kids a little bit more like what they are, mostly dumb teenagers with too many hormones and not enough sense yet, because we were all like that and we all grew up and look back at how dumb we were.

'Remember, they are kids. They will mess up, but just keep them safe and don't try find some deeply rooted issue to be the reason they rebel, it's mostly just because they want to try new things and want to look cool for the cute girl or hot guy in their class.'

The Village admin response to this was that kids were mostly robust, but, as in all things, balance had to be maintained. When there is a shambles playing out, someone has to keep an eye on it. This is called parenting. Most kids need healthy boundaries and consequences, but not hysteria and anxiety in overdrive. Nor neglect, she wrote. 'Balance. Always balance.'

As **Kate Gerber-Furmie** said: 'Some of the things that teens get into are par for the course. Depending on genetics and circumstances, some of the more mundane things can become very serious things. It is important to find balance. But to know that for the very reason kids can be dumb about stuff, there are very real dangers everywhere. It can take only a moment to change the course of their lives.'

Bryan Douglas-Henry responded: 'We too were all delinquent teens at some point […] trying to find ourselves in that horrible journey of pubescence. Thanks for the reminder to first put myself in my own shoes before I pull my tween aside and have a word.'

Michelle Mattee said: 'As a once wayward teen myself, I know that all I can do is make sure I educate as much as I can, stay open and honest, and be available when I need to be. Whether it's a heartfelt convo, or some understanding after a hard lesson, I hope my kids know that I'm there for them no matter what. I often feel incredibly grateful that my teen hasn't yet gotten up to any of the mischief and nonsense I was doing well before I was his age. There's still time though ... 😬 Parenting is such a fun adventure 🦴

Cheryl Gleeson-Baird's suggestion is that love will allow your child to come to you at any time, no matter how big the mistake they have made. 'Remember love them not their behaviour. Learning from our mistakes and moving forward, is the biggest life lesson that we can give our children.'

Vanessa says

There are so many posts from parents in this group wondering urgently what they can do to get their children out of the mess the family is currently in. I had coffee with a friend this weekend whom I know has tried everything to help her daughter, who is deep in the midst of the fireworks-and-fuckery years. (F&F is the term I use. Please forgive the profanity, but you know, sometimes, only profanity will do to describe parenting a teen. Sigh.)

Anyway. My thought is this, gleaned from many, many years hovering over this Village, hearing everyone's private thoughts, fears and dreams: sometimes, the best thing to do is just be there.

If you can afford help, yes, of course, throw all the professional help you can at it. Don't be proud; ask for and take all the help you get. Try many different versions of help. Don't give up. But sometimes, the most powerful, most effective, most hope-filled tool for getting a youngster through the storm is one predictable, reliable, solid adult. Just one. Not offering any answers, even, but offering a shoulder, an ear, an arm, belief and hope.

In my own stumbling through in those years, I thought I had to solve things for my kids. Make the bad stuff go away. I used to say, 'You can't protect your child, but you can equip them'.

These days, I don't say that at all. Nothing any parent can do can prepare any child for the slings and arrows that will come for them. But a scary world just feels more conquerable if you have an unshakeable someone who loves you and believes in you at your side. Being that person is obviously not easy: sticking to a script of belief, and faith in a kid's eventual survival and success, is hard when you're in the midst of the F&F. Some days you have to fake it. Stick a smile on your face. Use your words carefully.

You may even say nothing at all.

But if you listen, and acknowledge, and just be there – if you just stay steady – that could be all the superpowers a kid needs. Everyone needs one rock to cling to. And they don't always need or expect that rock to have the answers.

I found discovering this little life truth profoundly liberating. It's freeing not to have to know what to do all the time. Parents don't need the answers. We just need the love. And the faith in our kids. And we need to stick around. xxx

Cindy van der Merwe once wrote a message of hope for parents in the middle of the hard stuff: 'I remember a stage when I too used to become totally overwhelmed at times. As we get older and our teenagers grow into their own we realize that it's okay. We done good … we survived, and so did they.'

Staying safe when going out

Vanessa says

There's no such thing as a safe night out, but …

One of the reasons our teens are so unsafe when they venture out is because their peers are not equipped to take care of them. The social worlds of girls, for instance, is an unstable, complicated and political place. As parents, we may believe that our kids' only chance of safety when they go out is in numbers.

Sadly, this may not be so. Any group of teenage girls can be fractured, rife with politics that would put Game of Thrones *to shame. These groups involve popularity maths of which parents can be totally unaware. Ground Zero for teen girls, the most difficult and dangerous time to keep our kids safe, occurs at about the same time as their desire to appear grown up before they're ready for it and their withdrawal of comms with their parents.*

If your child is an outsider, a hanger-on, someone who has unknowingly offended someone, their situation is almost certainly more perilous. On nights out, there could be fights, squabbles over boys, bad choices ... even best friends make naïve decisions that could end up in disaster.

In a fantasy world, a buddy system is in play – but in my experience, it rarely is. As a parent, you have to accept that there will be times when no one in the group is sensible or streetwise. So, you need to plan accordingly. My suggestions?

- *Insist on Find My Phone or similar. Make having the app on at all times a condition of their going out. Keep an eye on it through the night.*
- *Tell your child to WhatsApp you when they arrive, when they move on, when they get back, if they're not coming home to you. Be a pain. Be unpopular. Interfere. When they're 18, you will have to step back. Until then, you need to be present. This is one case in which my laissez-faire attitude does not hold.*
- *Take your daughters* and *sons to self-defence classes. Even if what they learn there doesn't help, it could switch on some awareness, which may just make the difference.*
- *Tell your kids to be aware of the danger of muggings. Tell them to stay in the light. Never to walk alone. Always to be aware of what's going on around them. To keep their hand on their bag or cell phone. Not to walk around looking at their phone. Not to fall for 'What's the time?' or 'Those are cool shoes.'*
- *Until they're 18, ask for a cell phone number of at least one*

- friend with whom they'll be out. Preferably, get numbers of all the friends, so that you if can't get hold of your child you can check in via someone else.
- Teach your children how to go out responsibly. Telling them not to drink is a waste of time. Rather tell them not to take drinks from strange men or boys, no matter how flattered they are by the attention. Tell them to sip their drink slowly.
- Tell them that if they ever feel strange, in any way, to call you immediately. If you suspect they won't, out of shame or embarrassment, tell them to call an older sibling or a family member they trust.
- Assure them that they will not be judged or punished for drinking. Teenagers drink; there is almost no way to avoid this. Better to help them cope with it than to have them lie to you about it.
- More teens will get into trouble by drinking too much or mixing their drinks than by having a drink spiked. Unfortunately, though, both are possibilities. Suggest your teen drinks less, drinks slowly, that they never leave their drink unattended. Tell them to drink cider, not vodka. Tell them to drink water between drinks. Tell them you won't be angry if they phone when they feel insecure, or even tipsy. Reassure them of this every time they go out. They are scared of your rage, of disappointing or angering you.
- Tell them to call you at no matter what time, no matter where they are.
- Pick them up from parties. For the 15- to 16-year-olds, do not encourage sleepovers after parties. Sadly, very bad things happen when alcohol is involved and lights are off. If there have to be sleepovers, have them in your house and be present.
- Tell them to trust no one. How I wish this wasn't so, but it is.
- Tell them never to leave one of their own behind. This happens more often than you can imagine.

- *Tell them that, if they feel any of their friends are in danger, never to think it's not cool to interfere. Rather, they should ask the friend, 'Are you okay?' This could be crucial for keeping a friend safe.*

Reading between the lines (and sometimes just the lines) of the thousands of DMs I have received in the years of The Village's existence, I often pick up enormous worry, guilt, fear and sadness as a parent faces the fact that their child is not, at that moment, the robust, happy, healthy and thriving youngster, we all believe it is our duty to raise. None of these adjectives are accurate descriptions of the average teenager. Or human being, for that matter.

You can be both brave and fearful. Battered and beautiful, bruised and unbowed. You can be both a wonderful parent and have a child who appears to be careening off the rails. You can make many mistakes and still do a good job. You can have a rocky adolescence and a successful life. If your child is happy and healthy today, cherish the moment. Tomorrow is another day.

If they're struggling, get help. Parent. Believe in their future.

I know kids who've suffered sexual and mental abuse, poverty, uncertainty, the breakdown of families. I know kids who have behaved appallingly with serious consequences for their futures. I know kids who have serious mental health issues to contend with, their own or those of people close to them. Many of those kids have grown up to be my friends, colleagues, role models and inspirations.

So, when you witness your child's sadness, loneliness, alienation, depression, or anxiety, or if you discover they have an eating disorder or are cutting themselves, taking drugs, acting out, getting into proper trouble, failing at school, please don't think they are a failure – or that you are. To a large extent, this stuff cannot be prevented. As parents, our job is to help our children *find their own path. We cannot, and must not, dream of waving a wand to give them a painless existence. We are parents, not Gandalf the wizard.*

One constant indicator of a child's ability to cope in future, though, is *within our grasp. I've namedropped before that I was lucky enough to be in a business partnership with Oprah Winfrey. When I had my second child, I asked her for one piece of advice. 'It only takes one human being to be the difference in any child's life,' she said. 'We all can make that decision to be that human being.'*

But what kind of wisdom do you need to be that person? First, do not try to solve problems for a child. Our job is to support them, no matter how small they are, to support themselves. Second, get them the professional help they need. Move heaven and earth to get a child in distress to someone who understands the bigger picture. A child who has psychological support early becomes an adult who has much more powerful emotional literacy and weaponry to tackle the rest of the roller coaster. Be patient. It takes ages to forge strength. Nothing needs to be fixed this minute. Small steps at the child's side often do the job. Do not fear medication or the stigma of admitting that your kid is struggling. Asking for and receiving help is no failure. Never stop believing. Be a rock. Listen. Acknowledge. Don't wish it was over.

For the parents who ask for help and don't get a magic wand

Vanessa says

Sometimes, parent and child try several things that seem to make limited 'progress', or none at all. One step forward, two slipping sideways, three steps back (scroll through social media posts celebrating other people's kids getting a scholarship to Oxford, winning surfing competitions, representing the country in debating, getting a book published, or even just being smiley and healthy and with washed hair FFS, then lie down on the floor and weep quietly next to a large glass full of wine).

It can be scary and lonely here, I know. You try everything you can, but your child does not respond academically, socially or psychologically in a way that allows you to relax, breathe out, tell yourself you're doing ' a good job', that you're a 'good parent'.

On these days, it's helped me to remember that I'm not meant to 'fix' my kids. When you think about it, 'fixing' other humans to our satisfaction would be a spectacularly narcissistic thing to do. Our kids are as entitled to own and learn from their own struggles as they are to learn from their own successes or solutions. And their own solutions may not manifest conveniently: some positive change happens imperceptibly, especially when viewed from too close to get a proper perspective. In the end, our kids are ours only briefly. Sometimes, stepping back, finding a way to believe in your child, to focus on their unique characteristics rather than on their flaws and challenges, is the most supportive thing you can do.

Hopeful and helpful

Chapter 12

RAISING CITIZENS TO BE PROUD OF

Unless we run a family business in crime, most of us hope our children will be *good* people – that they will respect people and property, be honest, work hard, show kindness and practise tolerance even with the most trying people.

Being a good *citizen* takes being a good *person* a little further.

Theodore Roosevelt said a good citizen was one who was prepared to pull their own weight, and not be a 'mere passenger'. This person would have a capacity for self-help and regard for the rights of others. Roosevelt did not extend these rights to animals. He was a hunter who killed for fun and mowed down some of Africa's greatest animals in the name of 'sport'. Many of The Villagers' vegan children would *definitely not* approve of him and probably not care what he has to say about what it means to be a good citizen – which just shows how well many of us are doing at turning out not just good people, but good citizens. It also shows how collective values change over time.

Today's teens are better trained to be critical of the world they have inherited than we ever were. Villager **Darryl Lampert** wrote: 'I think most kids grow up with a far stronger sense of [advocacy for themselves and others] than what we had as kids or possibly have now – at least that has been my experience.'

Rules, rights and responsibilities

Villager **Natasha Reeler** says she teaches her children the following things in the hope that they will become good citizens:
- 'Always choose kindness
- Give more than you take
- Honesty & acceptance always
- Check your privilege
- There are always 3 sides to a story
- Pay it forward where you can.'

Being a good citizen means first and foremost understanding that there are rules, and most children begin to learn this at home and then at school. As they develop, they should also develop a critical awareness of when rules are good and when they are bad.

Morality and ethics

A discussion on The Village about underage drinking shows the kinds of moral and philosophical problems we have to wrestle with as parents.

It's a complex subject, but the participants debate it the way we have to debate with our children about what it means to be a good citizen.

(For the record, it is against the law to drink before the age of 18 in South Africa. The riskiest time for developing alcohol addiction is thought to be the teen years, and it is generally thought that it is healthiest to not begin drinking until 18.)

'The law is the law ... if we teach kids it's ok to choose which law to break because it's not such a big deal, we will have bigger problems ahead of us!!' – **Starrene Stuart**

'And what about the laws in North Korea? Should we blindly follow and accept things just because it's the law?' – **Roxanne Van Der Schyff**

'I'm sorry I'm not budging on this one ... kids need to respect and adhere to the law. I have a 17 year old. I am trying my best to bring him up to be a law-abiding citizen. Letting kids decide what law to ignore is looking for trouble ... and North Korea does not care 2 hoots about SA. If we cannot follow a simple law as no underage drinking we have a problem.' – **Starrene Stuart**

'I disagree. Not that long ago in SA we had some very disturbing laws that everyone had to follow. I prefer raising my kids to think for themselves, know their limits and be street smart rather than following laws blindly.' – **Roxanne Van Der Schyff**

'I know all about those laws, I was affected by them, but the issue here is underage drinking, a fundamental law which I PERSONALLY think is a good law. It's there for a reason. If one is not happy about the laws, go about it the legal way. It's not for you or me to say, she/he is 15, she can drink because I am with her or they can handle it! We need kids to adhere and respect the law. If they unhappy about it, help them change it the right way!!' – **Starrene Stuart**

Does everyone belong and have a right to engage and contribute in South Africa?

South Africa's experience with democracy has been shaky and many of the day-to-day social problems our children face have to do with race and privilege.

Noëleen Bruton said she had two daughters who weren't quite teens yet, and who she was actively bringing up to be sensitive and caring.

'As South Africans I make sure that we don't avoid but discuss the ills of apartheid and the importance of not judging people on the basis of the colour of their skin. Whenever issues of racism have arisen – be it at school or in the media we discuss it in detail ... how hurtful it is, how wrong it is and why white South Africans need to acknowledge the past and actively work towards rectifying these imbalances. Here's my dilemma: I don't want my daughters growing up thinking that there is no place for them in this country. I want them to be proud of who they are whilst at the same time taking responsibility for the past. How do I instil confidence, a sense of belonging and a sense of responsibility (for the past and the privilege they do indeed have) whilst at the same time not letting them be influenced into believing that they need to leave SA to have a future? It sometimes feels as if SA is like an 'incubator' country. What do I do to teach them they have a responsibility but they themselves are not guilty due to the past, that they need to love and invest in this country?'

Futhi Nhlengethwa responded: 'You are probably already doing it. The fact that you are asking the question means you are parenting them consciously ... keep it up.'

Sarah Oosthuizen wrote: 'I love your heart to raise compassionate girls! I think a big issue underlying our growing 'incubator' world-view is the real-life social-disconnect amongst South Africans. I've found so much goodwill amongst races – and a lot of graciousness toward us as the privileged ones. It's easier said than done, but by getting involved in other communities (specifically finding organisations where you are not the 'benevolent giver', but more equal) your girls will find the common humanity between cultures.

'My kids were part of a social circus for 5 years, where no one was given privileges, and it was a safe way to foster friendships as equally as possible in our horribly divided society.

'There are safe places to find your place in spaces that feel "foreign": libraries and Think Tanks, dance groups, places where your kids can learn skills in environments away from the suburbs.

'You will find that the negativity about our country feels smaller as you find kids and families who just want the same sense of community and compassion that you do.'

Karin says

An understanding of rules naturally leads to learning about rights: your own and others' rights. What are the rights, for instance, of teachers to a safe working environment? What is your own right to wear a headscarf to school? To not be bullied? Do you have the right to continue going to school if you are pregnant?

In turn, the learning of rights leads to the understanding of personal responsibility, which often leads to action and engagement. A lack of action and engagement can often lead to feelings of hopelessness and helplessness, which can lead to depression and anxiety.

Active citizenship is not only an expression of hope for a better world and a better future for everyone, but a means by which we can dispel the demons that haunt us in the middle of the night.

Ulandy Gribble had this to say on The Village: 'Children mirror what they see. There's a massive difference us as parents can do to raise our own awareness and sensitivity. While playing taxi to a group of girls recently, one of the girls pipes up at the sight of a person begging at the robot "Why does he not just go work?" This has stuck with me. Parents – it's all of us that need to make a difference, not our kids.'

Celeste Fortuin wrote: 'Awareness is important. I have a diverse family – none of us have the 'same' skin colour, which has interesting ideas of how they perceive themselves; and I find that what has become equally important for my kids, are their class and gender identities. Dealing with privilege in these areas is the topic of the day … I am having wonderful conversations with my male-bodied child about male privilege, and how the body s/he is in can signal privilege and oppression to many female-bodied persons. On a lighter note, though, I find that this new generation has found interesting ways to deal with diversity, something that still does not come that easy for us who grew up during Apartheid. There is definitely hope for our next generation, and I must just always caution myself to confront my own prejudices, and not pass it on to my children. Basic values such as love, respect, kindness, empathy, non-discrimination and non-sexism, these I don't hesitate to reinforce in them though ✧'

The Village leads the way

Lockdown and loadshedding were, for many of us Villagers, the most intense lesson we will ever get in our own puniness. We realised we could not control the world. We cannot make it *not* be bad, we cannot make it *not* hurt us and our families. The shock of this has been life-changing for many. Some of us have been tipped into an abyss of never-ending worry of such an extreme nature that we drink more, sleep less and shout unexpectedly at our partners or children.

Many of us, though, have come through the crushing reality of our own powerlessness to keep the world ticking away nice and orderly, and we found our own wonky ways to embrace the world as it is. This too is an act of good citizenship. We pick up our load. We walk our path. We take a bag off someone who is buckling under the weight they are carrying for as long or short as we can.

We reach out: Villagers send matric dresses and suits (and even matric dance partners!) to families that need them. We offer massages, second-hand phones, data top-ups and food packages to people on the other side of the country.

We make sandwiches for Ladles of Love; we send out compost to suburban food gardens; we do free graphic design for NGOs.

We give time. We give energy. We give kindness and understanding.

The Village is a place that daily demonstrates the very best of what it means to be a good citizen.

Good citizenship is power.

Sue Segar says her children grew up with her husband saying to them, '"The world is tough and fascinating but tough and unfair. Why not just engage with it?" Rather than be passive, engage. It has turned out to be great advice for both my kids.'

Good citizenship can happen in roughly three categories: participatory citizenship, justice-oriented citizenship and responsibility-oriented citizenship.

Here are the ways in which Village parents lead their children towards active citizenship.

Participatory citizenship

Humans are more wired towards helping than hurting. There is a lot of science to back this up. For that reason, participatory citizenship may be the one that comes to us and that we show our children most easily. It includes:
1. Giving our time, energy or talent to events, actions and causes that will not enrich us directly
2. Recycling properly and thoughtfully, and reducing the use of single-use plastic
3. Donating blood
4. Composting
5. Picking up litter
6. Leading or helping to organise actions to change what is bad and improve what can be improved
7. Collecting things that are needed by organisations that aid, assist, feed, care for, or train people
8. Contributing to emergency responses during fire and flood and other disasters.

Justice-oriented citizenship

This kind of involvement with society means that you see beyond your immediate realm of influence to the architecture our society is built on. For instance, like **Ulandy Gribble** pointed out previously, it means that you see that someone is not *choosing* to beg for money because they can't be bothered to work.

Justice-oriented citizenship means that you understand that individual people aren't the only ones responsible for how their lives turn out, but that economic and political forces have an influence that can't always be balanced by your own efforts to improve yourself. This kind of citizenship:
1. Is aware of different kinds of privilege and how they manifest in society

2. Has a strong idea of personal values, like a sense of fairness, and wants to see these reflected in the world
3. Believes strongly in respect and practises tolerance towards people who are not like you, however hard it is to find common ground with these people
4. Understands the difference between equality and equity. This is what it is: equality means that every person and every group of people is given the same opportunities and the same resources. Equity recognises that every person has different circumstances, so it may mean that some people need more resources and opportunities to reach an equal outcome.

Where does good citizenship begin?

Our children become good citizens with or without our help, but their environment will, like most things, influence who they choose to become as adults.

If they see community involvement modelled, they will take it as a given that it is how we live, as much as we tidy our houses or take our pets for walks. If they see us taking voting seriously, they will vote. If they see us working through a tricky ethical issue with our partners, they'll know polarised, rigid thinking doesn't always serve us, and that nuance is not the enemy.

Most parents use the modelling method, but Villager **Anne Taylor** notes: 'I always thought [teaching these things] "by example" would work. But I have come to realise one must be far more explicit about the things one cares about. It's talk, talk, talk that's got to happen.'

Responsible citizenship

We need good information to be good citizens.

There are things we can do to train ourselves and our children to fully take up our responsibilities as citizens of a world that is shared with many other people and creatures. These things make for fantastic family discussions over long lunches. (Remember to keep discussion respectful and open. Don't mock or diminish opinions you don't like. Ask questions. Allow the quieter ones in the family to join in. Be curious, not judgemental.)

1. **Critical thinking.** Just because something has 'always been like this', it doesn't mean it's being done the right way, or in a way that considers all the ways of being in the world. Why, for instance, is Christmas a holiday for everyone, but Eid isn't? Our duty towards our children is to listen to their questions openly and allow those questions to open us. Our duty is not to have all the answers, but to encourage the questions and the thinking skills.
2. **Ethical assessments.** These are great for dinner table discussions, and they promote critical thinking. Is it okay to steal an apple if you're hungry? If there's no parking, and you're late for a meeting, is it okay to park on a red line? How does my right to self-determination fit into broader rights? Is it okay for the girls to be allowed to wear trousers to school, but for the boys not to be allowed to wear skirts?
3. **Laws and governance.** How are laws made? What is a municipality's role in the state healthcare system? Can private schools make their own rules about who they will or will not educate? Should dogs be on leads in public? Should we vote even if it feels like it makes no difference?
4. **Advocacy.** How do we advocate for what we believe is right? How do we advocate for ourselves? How do we advocate for others without muscling in and taking over?
5. **Science literacy.** We must understand the formal concepts of intellectual inquiry so that we can distinguish between myth, opinion and fact in order to make the best decisions we can make. How is scientific inquiry practised and regulated and what does that mean for how we can understand

the bewildering world? How do we reconcile our religious ideas with scientific fact? Do the two things have to cancel one another out?
6. **Media literacy.** For us to be able to educate ourselves about all these things, we need to understand how to read the media in a way that protects us from misinformation and fear. We have to be able to understand bias, the role of money in the production of information, the basic ethics of responsible journalism, how to read a variety of points of view from reliable media with different assessments, and how to find out which media are reliable. Who do we go to for the best possible information? How do we know if information is correct? What are peer-reviewed studies? And, although we are still in its early days, how are we going to train ourselves to see whether something is human or machine-made? If we aren't allowed to steal other people's intellectual property at school or university, why is AI allowed to do so?

Sue Segar, who is married to the well-known investigative journalist Martin Welz, wrote: 'Even though M and I are both journos, it is [our children] who have a much better sense of what is fake and what is not! I've often seen [my son] dash through to M's office and say 'You'd better delete that tweet, your engaging with a bot!'

Darryl Lampert said: 'As far as sorting out fake news, you can guide them when they come to you with fake news but you can also teach them to read news from multiple sources across the spectrum before making up their minds about something. The reality is that they have also taught us about good scientific sites and what can be trusted. As far as governance and laws, teach them by example – if you are law-abiding and ethical that will be their best guide.'

Other things that make you an even better citizen of households, communities, the country and the world

- First aid
- Knowing how to manage your money
- Consuming less
- Awareness of the saviour complex
- How to respond to trauma as it is happening
- Hope
- Self-care
- Self-regulation.

Hope

Part of being a good citizen is often seeking and finding hope in our environments and in ourselves, and keeping alive the flames of justice and a better world for everyone.

Alexandra Souchon wrote: 'Hope is a miniscule seed, the size of a mustard seed. Every one of us has been gifted this measure of hope. If we misappropriate our hope, it makes our hearts sick. Makes sense to retrieve it from where we put it to putting it in a wiser, more eternal, higher purpose. If the next generation is our future, then I need as much help as I can possibly glean to invest into them and our collective future.'

To some degree (barring those who don't have the luxury of data for Facebook), The Village is a microcosm of this complex country we call home. Despite the many offers of advice, the practical help, the support, the laughs, the friendships that have developed, the sense of community, the stories of hope and triumph, there are also days when it seems like problems are the only thing the world has to offer.

What hope is

From a dictionary definition perspective, hope is 'a feeling that what is wanted can be had or that events will turn out for the best'. That's succinct and accurate, but it doesn't capture the feeling's weightiness enough.

Hope isn't just necessary. It's essential to life. A lack of hope can – it often does – lead to death – to suicide, family murders and large-scale, life-sapping and soul-destroying despair. Hope is for life. Hope is the very opposite of words that begin with 'de': despair, despondency, derangement, decay, degradation, descent, death.

Because our lives revolve around young people, we have to find ways to foster hope. It's the responsible thing to do. For *their* sakes.

Why hope is important

If you have ever spent a solid amount of time with someone who only ever sees the dark side of life, you will have been given a glimpse of how important hope is. You can come away from an interaction like that feeling like everything is terrible and that nothing is worthwhile. It's an awful feeling.

If you had the inner resources to overcome the pull of the black hole that surrounds people like that, you will know the relief you feel when you have been able to resist being sucked into it. Hopelessness is a dark and sticky place.

Hope is not delusion or avoidance. It's not ignoring the trouble. It's seeing the trouble and looking beyond it. It's not puppy-dog optimism. It's not being a pain-in-the-ass Pollyanna. It's not about ending sad conversations with 'love and light' as though the words 'love and light' are a spell that make depression disappear.

Hope is not passive

Hope is not wishing you get a better job; it's updating your CV and sending it out.

Hope is not watching the litter pile up by the hedge at the park and hoping someone will clean it; it's taking a black bag and some gloves next time you go.

Hope is not stressing about your child's ability to cope with low-level bullying at school. It's talking to them to help find out how they think you could help them.

There's this weird thing about hope: it requires you to do something, (listen more deeply, pay better attention, change your online habits, draw up a budget, reach out to someone you haven't spoken to in a while) and then, in return, it gives you more of itself. It works on a kind of a loop that reminds you that you are not without some power, however limited that power is, which can fill up your energy tank and make you have more hope.

Science indicates that people who actively engage with some useful activities during and after there's been a disaster – think of the floods in KZN, the drought in the Eastern and Western Cape, the destructive fires that have wiped out people's homes – are making good use of their stress hormones. Doing something like collecting blankets or making sandwiches helps us to sidestep the less helpful stress responses like fight, flight or freeze. Activity helps restore the body to a sense of purpose and agency. It gives you the power to feel less useless.

Where Villagers get their hope

Action

'Action gives me hope. Doing something about it.' – **Pam Marsh**

'In times of crisis, I look for the helpers. They give me enormous hope. Be it the feeding schemes, those helping animal, our oceans and rivers, [people standing up against] gender-based violence ... the list goes on. Helping the helpers gives me hope and purpose.' – **Julia Doveton-Cain**

Children

'My kids. Seriously, every time I ever considered quitting, they were my reason to get up and get at it.' – **Dirk van Niekerk**

'My children and my grandchildren.' – **Jacoba Louw**

'Watching children from incredibly dark backgrounds rise and conquer. Kids abused, neglected, forgotten, forsaken, blossoming with just some love and consistency. Over and over and over again. Realising that in the youth in our country is so much power – so much more than we adults have! You cannot possibly miss the hope in these stories! And I get to watch that every day ... how lucky am I?' – **Tiffini Hein**

Perspective shifts

'Go back to the simple things. Literally stop and smell the roses. Just be present in those small moments.' – **Kaolin Thomson**

'I take a good look at how far I've come and also how far others have made it and then I will tell myself if I or they made it this far then I know I can go further. I always believe in being hopeful even when it's hard as there are always moments of happiness and joy that keep me going. My hope is believing in the best outcome.' – **Carmen Andries**

'The fact that the Universe has my back. Everything is exactly as it should be, and hard times are a step on the journey. Events that occur happen for me, not to me. It's a mind switch, but it gives me enormous hope.' – **Jo Styles Worthington-Smith**

'By taking my focus off something singular, I expand my view. It takes me out of my rational brain into a greater space of awe. Life is magical. Learning to be present in the moment is key! Just be here now and soak up the loveliness. Also, the concept of being a creator and not a survivor. When I worry, I choose to take that energy and put it into creating my future. I build pictures and feast on the emotions. It helps the subconscious align and work toward something, as opposed to just surviving in a loop.' – **Laura Carmen Middleton**

'What gives me hope: when I look back on times in my life where the situation seemed bleak, yet the eventual outcome was positive.

Examples are: my husband's mental health struggles that he conquered. My fertility battle yet now I have two healthy children. I have an unshakable optimistic outlook based on how my life has turned out.' – **Alison Roberts Theron**

'Focusing on stories of amazing people who overcame challenges or did great things with their lives. Reminding myself that it's only going to be hard for a season. Learn what I can while I'm in it. Looking back at where I've been gives perspective when the road ahead looks too far away. The idea that circumstances are always going to get better – even though there isn't any proof at the time – is largely because it was instilled in me by my mother from a very young age. Our parent's words really do become our inner voice when we get older. Ultimately the gift of hope was passed down to me.' – **Cindy Naude**

Gratitude

'We count our blessings and take action.' – **Philippe Samouilhan**

'One word: gratitude. I say a sort of gratitude prayer every morning when I have my tea. It's become a habit. I list a few things every morning (they need to be different things every day) that I'm grateful for and I basically say thanks. It's also a constant state of mind – living "in the moment". And yes, I have to remind myself most days, as I get off track easily. But I'm getting there. It has helped so much.' – **Allison Capes Gibson**

'Be grateful for what you have. Gratitude is the highest frequency and when you live from this place it is not possible to feel anxiety or fear. Wherever you place your focus expands, so focus on what you want to create more of and less of what you do. Surround yourself with people who support and uplift you versus the complainers, the negative nancies and naysayers. You've got to get very clear on what you want out of life and focus on that place, surrendering that everything is always working out for your highest good.' – **Diane Hill**

'Focusing on my blessings, at time literally naming things out loud that I am thankful for.' – **Nicolette Pretorius**

Connection with others and faith

'My faith in God [to whom I turn first]. My family, who I am fortunate to be able to say are wonderful, genuine people. My daughter, who has her life ahead of her and who will make an impact on learners. My friends, who are a precious part of my life, the ones I see often as well as the friends I only see now and again. The Village (and I really mean this) who come through time and time again for strangers. The beautiful creatures I see in my garden every day.' – **Tania Slade**

'Relationships. Very happily married. Love my kids. Wonderful sister. Fabulous, supportive colleagues. Good friends. Cheerful strangers. Life goes on. We are all in it together.' – **Laurel Giddy**

A little bit of everything

'Being at the receiving end of a kind gesture gives me hope; being in nature and being able to marvel at it gives me hope; synchronicity gives me hope, when the planets align and something good happens to people who deserve it. Mastering a new skill gives me hope; when love is reciprocated gives me hope. When I navigate a painful day, I feel hopeful; the exuberance of my dog's greeting when I get home from work gives me hope; seeing my children grapple with life and find their way gives me hope. Also, watching friends – who've known deep tragedy – not give up on life! That gives me hope. And people who can forgive and love with grace, they give me hope.' – **Sharon Sorour-Morris**

Karin says

To live holding both the terrifying and unjust in mind while at the same time finding strength to do the drone work of living is a juggling act we perform with various degrees of success at different times of our lives. Sometimes, when our juggling is going well, we even manage to access a rebellious, subversive joy. Here are some of the medicines in my imaginary self-doctoring bag. They're not particularly original, but they come through for me every single time the darkness of the world becomes oppressive:

1. *Whenever the proverbial apocalyptic shit hits the proverbial fan – war, famine, flood, plague – I remember that this is when **ordinary people become extraordinary**. Think of how people rally around – even you, you rally around – when domestic calamities beset others. When things become mega-kak, more people seem to become mega-amazing.*
2. ***Focus on the makers.** Comedians, acrobats, app designers, glass blowers, inventors, film makers, illustrators, song writers, novelists, painters, sculptors – and all the other kinds of makers I haven't named – know how to turn nothing into something and often they make things that simply stun all the crappy feelings about the crappy side of the world right out of me.*
3. ***Work.** I know not everyone loves their work as much as I love mine, so it might not be a feasible escape, but when I'm working, I can lose myself in it. Plus, it is a form of making. As long as I am making, I'm too distracted to notice the gloom all around. Work also tends to drag in its wake a happy collection of flotsam and jetsam: fertile collaboration, new ideas, and the brick-by-brick construction of something that is ongoingly and ultimately rewarding. I also find that money I earn myself, however little it is, by the sweat of my very own brave brow, always makes me feel competent and satisfied with my own sense of self-worth, which boosts my sense of agency. So that's an extra bonus.*
4. ***Physical effort.** I find it hard to ruminate when I am out of breath, tangled in a yoga pose, hiking up an incline or dancing around the kitchen table. Extra points to physical effort for a) production of short-term psychoactive effects that make you feel calmer and b) the long-term effects on your general health and well-being.*
5. ***Connect with strangers.** Sounds weird, but I get an incredible high from connecting with people I meet in my everyday life.*

Most people are really nice and I find that so many South Africans just have this instant default mode to laughter, which might be the only thing we truly have in common with one another across all our many divides. During authentic connections, however fleeting, people will often afford you glimpses of their own rich lives, negating the tendency we have to slip too far down into our own dramas.

6. **Don't make it worse for others.** *Don't bitch and moan. I realise we all do it sometimes, but it needs to be taken in hand because moaning has a visceral effect on other people. I try to keep a lid on it when it seems like the world is irredeemably ghastly because there is no possible way that moaning is going to make anyone or anything better. In fact, I feel that the best thing to do, for myself and for people around me, is to notice the good things.*
7. **Do something to make the world around you better.** *This is especially important when it feels like the things that are wrong are way bigger than me – like systems of terror and oppression, or climate change. Feeling like I have some agency to make some minuscule difference helps me enormously.*

We must always remember too: Nolite te bastardes carborundorum! *Which means: Don't let the bastards grind you down.*

Chapter 13

DO AS YOU WOULD BE DONE BY

In life, we know, there are no guaranteed second chances. What we *can* do is try to do better for our children than was done to us when we were young.

This isn't a perfect solution, of course. Our children's lives, as we have said before, are not convenient mirror images of our own. But looking back at our younger selves and trying to find a golden thread of lessons learnt resulted in a beautiful thread of valuable insights into how we parent our own children, from almost 300 Villagers.

Of course, no amount of hindsight seems to help us in the moment. *That* moment, when all wisdom, patience and experience desert us and we are left lost, yelling, snapping, or ... just making the wrong bloody decision. The kind of moment that comes back to haunt us years later when we face the inevitable parenting report card from our children:

'You always made me feel uncomfortable about my weight.'

'I was too ashamed to tell you I was drunk the night that ...'

'You were tougher on me than on my brother and sister.'

'You spent so much time working, you had no idea what was going on with us.'

Every child, it seems, is a *highly* skilled scorekeeper of parental injustice, with a forensic and laser-sharp memory for wrongs suffered at the hands of Mom and Dad. (Consider your relationship with your own parents for a minute. In your child role, you are this scorekeeper too!) Because, of course, the inescapable guarantee of the parenting experience is that you *will* get it wrong.

Not for the parents of tweens, teens or young adults the luxury of the cliché 'You don't have to be a perfect parent, you are perfect to your child'. Our lot is a much more humble and – dare I say – authentic one. But that doesn't make any of us bad parents. What stumbling through makes us, of course, is human beings.

It's not perfection that makes us good parents. It's not never making mistakes. What *does* have a chance of making us decent parents is a commitment to trying to be better. It's empathy, humility and open-mindedness; a willing spirit to continue to learn, to change, to *reach* our kids. The most powerful way to do this, perhaps, is to connect with our own younger selves, to remember what it was like to be someone's tricky, naughty, misunderstood child, bursting with potential and possibility, ourselves. What would we have liked to know? What would have helped us learn? What would we share with our own children, now?

A gift from The Village to you and your children: The advice we'd give our younger selves

'If I could say one thing to my young self? I'd say "Feel no shame". No one worthwhile is watching you with nastiness; no one worthwhile is laughing at or judging you. Be free. It took me a LONG time to walk into a room without feeling inadequate. Now I walk into any rooms, anywhere.' – **Vanessa Raphaely**

'No need to kneel to anyone, stand your ground: you are worth it.' – **Kay Oosthuizen**

'Don't cry or show how much the name calling hurts. Laugh and pretend you don't care. Your tears give them power over you.' – **Jennifer Wyatt**

'You will realise your indomitable strength and fearlessness. Realise and celebrate your worth. Do not look to others to affirm the strength and inner beauty that is already a part of you. Be the warrior you are. Love yourself first.' – **Lesley Shireen Hector**

'Go on being fierce. For too long you were afraid to speak up, but you have now found your voice, use it wisely. Go and love those in your life with your whole heart, as you were meant to.' – **Tillie Smit**

'Don't be so frightened of failing that you stop trying new things. It's okay to fail. Because it teaches you how to get up again on the other side. You will never regret trying. Because who knows, you might have succeeded.' – **Kim Penstone**, admin

'I would tell myself to advocate harder for my voice to be heard. Every child deserves to be heard and believed when they speak out. And adults DO NOT always deserve "respect". This dangerous narrative must stop.' – **Nelia Geldenhuys**

'There's nothing wrong with you. Being unique and an individual is just not celebrated enough in this world. Don't be ashamed of who you are. Being neurodivergent is amazing! You add so much to this world and those around you.' – **Roelien Kruger**

'You are enough.' – **Wendy-Anne Hinson**

'It will take some time, but the day will come when you no longer fear him. Trust yourself, listen to the voice that tells you it's not ok. You are More Than, not Less.' – **Janine Naiker**

'Believe in yourself, believe you can do anything. And do it. Don't be timid. Don't allow words, said by others and said to yourself, to limit your dreams. Don't let insecurities rule decisions. Don't play safe, take the leap, take the risk. BE BRAVER THAN YOU FEEL.' – **Jillmaree Mitchell**

'Your childhood trauma will make you tender to the suffering of others, and your adult life will bear no resemblance to the horrors of your childhood. Although you'll spend the rest of your lives recovering, your adult lives will be full of extraordinary moments, many hurting souls will find safety in your homes, you'll do great things, you'll find your voice, and you'll be loved and warmly embraced everywhere you go.' – **Yanga Zembe Zondi**

'People will hurt you. You will experience trauma that no one should ever go through. Never let those events define you. You are worthy of love. Stay weird, kind and silly, despite what society makes you believe.' – **Luka van der Merwe**

'You have been taught to be the best version of yourself that your parents, teachers, and advisors could imagine. Question and possibly unlearn all of that and discover for yourself what truly makes your heart sing, what makes you feel powerful and yet comfortable in your own skin at the same time. Then it won't matter what anyone else thinks and you'll be free.' – **Janice Melmed**

'Where you come from does not matter, what matters is what you stand for.' – **Jane Wentzel**

'Just because the person who's supposed to be the protector isn't, doesn't mean you have to grow up right now. You deserve to be a child. Don't rush to grow up …' – **Meredith Haywood**

'Say yes to everything, don't be scared and go live your life the way you were meant to.' – **Diane Hill**

'Tell someone what is happening to you, you will get help. It is not your fault.' – **Lara Berman**

'Freckles are beautiful. Bad haircuts grow out. Fat cheeks are cute. Not all intelligences are measured in school. Embrace your quirkiness. You are worthy. You are enough. Be You.' – **Camilla Hazell**

'The world is so much bigger than what you see in front of you. The path laid out for you by others is not always the best path for you. Don't be impatient to find the right path, there's no such thing as a wrong turn.' – **Simone Cornelissen**

'Nothing lasts forever. Nothing. You'll learn this with time. The light and shadow: happiness and sorrow and the emotions between them. You'll suffer such loss it will drive you to despair: your heart will shatter and it won't mend perfectly but know that others have semi-mended hearts too, and their broken hearts feel as yours will, in time. The thing is with these stitched-back-together hearts, they still feel and they can love and they care and so often they survive. Yours will survive too.' – **Jill Hinchcliffe**

'Don't let your insecurities and self-doubt influence and limit your decisions in life. Follow your passion and dreams, believe in yourself and put yourself first now and then. It is ok to fail sometimes, no one expects you to do everything perfectly all the time. You're allowed to make mistakes, and if you do, get up and move on.' – **Sameera Wehr Kafaar**

'Don't make yourself small for other people's benefit. There will always be those that don't want you to shine. Shine anyway.' – **Yvette Bowden**

'NO is a full sentence.' – **Michelle Cilliers**

'Break the cycle. You have the power to change the world for the next generation. Let your voice be heard.' – **Evette Terblanche**

'Do not let the shame that those closest to you feel about you define you, stop you, dim you. Do not be quiet, do not be hidden, stand up! Stamp your foot! And shout "I AM HERE AND I AM EXCELLENT IN EVERY WAY" despite those who will treat you with judgement and with a lack of knowledge but mostly because of their own fears. Live in forgiveness because if you don't you will live tethered and chained. Forgiveness, kindness above all no matter your circumstances or who did what to you when. (It's irrelevant, and the energy it takes not to forgive is like a small death inside you.) Life is going to be so very hard, sad, tough, relentless – it will take you to your breaking point but do not be afraid as you were created perfectly and with love, kindness, forgiveness, joy, giving generously, gentleness, peace and an inner wisdom that will keep you upright and strong, the ability to dig down deep and keep going is in you and in all of us. Find your tribe sooner angel and accommodate no human that does not appreciate and love you completely for you. You are enough, beautiful child, you are enough.' – **Tamalyn Petch**

'Don't let the world make you hard. Gentleness and empathy are not weaknesses. Don't let yourself be made small. Do not minimise who you are for the convenience of others. Don't let them put you in a box, or take their judgment to heart if you don't fit in. Be authentic and true to yourself. Walk to the beat of your own drum. Don't listen to that little voice in your head telling you that you are not enough, and don't worry about who other people expect you to be. Go on the adventure. Try the new thing. Find joy in the small things. Put yourself first sometimes. Don't put off doing things until circumstances are better. Do them now. You were not born to fit in – you were born to stand out. You are smart, you are kind, you are worthy and yes, you are enough.' – **Lesley Scott**, admin

Chapter 14
BEST ADVICE EVER ...

'If there is one thing that being a Village admin has taught me, it is that regardless of our diversity, we have far more in common than we might think,' admin **Lesley Scott** posted on 1 January 2024. 'If we are able to look beyond our differences, we will find the uniting threads of our humanity.'

She continued, '2023 was a lot and people everywhere were going through the most. And yet ... The Village continued to show up.
- People were reunited.
- We helped people get their sick children home from abroad.
- New friendships were formed.
- We supported families that were in need.
- We gave love and understanding to people who felt misunderstood.
- We held up the lonely and the hurting.
- We followed some wild dating adventures and laughed at the exploits of our own Fiery Fiona.
- We reminisced, and shared our stories, and complained about the down-sides of ageing.
- We provided a spark of light at the end of many dark tunnels.
- We reassured parents and helped an uncle become a dad.

- Cakes were baked, bicycles gifted, clothing passed on.
- We helped the abused and vulnerable get to places of safety.
- We held space for those who received a scary health diagnosis.
- We celebrated one another's wins and consoled those who experienced losses.
- We helped a principal raise funds, but more importantly, we helped him to sow seeds of hope.
- We discussed sensitive topics with grace and broke the silence and stigma associated with mental illness.
- We remembered that everyone's life is unique and that there can be many ways of reaching our destination.
- We learned to be kinder, more accepting, and more inclusive (and that sometimes scrolling by was in everyone's best interest).
- We shared our recipes, recommended airfryers, and with small acts of kindness, one Villager's actions led to many families enjoying a tasty and nutritious Christmas lunch ...'

All that in one year. From this list, you can see that a lot of what happens on The Village is supporting adults – because we firmly believe that to support our tweens, teens and young adults, we need to support their parents. But The Village is primarily a place where people can ask the hard questions about parenting teens, and so, to end off, here is a list of some of the best advice given to and by the people who make up this incredible community.

Mantras to live by with teens

Celebrate their uniqueness

Try not to measure your child against others. Each individual has their strengths. The greatest gift you can give them is the opportunity to find their own, and the knowledge that that is enough for you, their parent.

'Each child is unique – guide them so they find their strengths and then set them free and hope the universe helps watch over them.'
– **Sarah Withey**

'Being good enough is good enough. Kids don't come with manuals, and if they did, it still would not be a one-size-fits-all! Best lesson I learnt from my more introverted daughter (who is actually an ambivert) is that extroverts believe that there is something wrong with introverts. There isn't. It's just a different way of being. Not wrong. Just different!' – **Jane Bradpiece Plit**

'Identify their passion and unique abilities and quietly support them to develop it. It might not be your dream or your passion. It might be something so obscure that you miss it (like taking machines apart). Then give them the tools they need to take it further. Don't be pushy. Let them find their own way. They may not be the strongest academically, socially or in sport, but they will always have their "thing" that they excel in, where they shine.' – **Karen Thorne**

'1. Give your kids the freedom to tap into their own passions and motivations when they're young, it will help a great deal when they get to high school and uni. 2. We have 18 summers or maybe 21 if we are lucky – make them count. 3. Practice the pause.' – **Khilona Radia**

'We bring these children into the world and we feed them, clothe them and nurture them but they are their own people and they are going to choose their path. Yes we can guide them and help them but ultimately they are going to be who they were born to be.' – **Sandy Martin Bradley**

'1. ENJOY your child. 2. Be kind above all else. 3. You are your child's inner voice so let that voice be a voice of love and support. 4. Each and every child is special and brings a special gift to the world – each gift should be celebrated.' – **Paula Ferreira Abel**

'Don't live through your child – and before you say you don't, take five minutes and think about it. Just because you envisage a future for your child it doesn't mean that your child wants the same thing. Don't make decisions on behalf of your child about their future – that may work when they're really young but by the time they become teenagers, it's not your decision to make.' – **Jacoba Louw**

Be there

In the busyness of running a home, career, friendships and families, lifting, making school lunches and general organised chaos, remember to give your tween, teen or young adult your focused time and the sense that their space at home is a safe one they can always come back to when the world gets too much.

'Play with your kids.' – **Ruth Thembani**

'1. I always fetch from a night out/party etc – then I know they are safe, kids can come sleep over, I find out fun stuff that's happened and keeps you in the loop. 2. When my child is sad and low, I ask 'Shall I climb in the hole with you, or do you want a ladder' – in other words, shall I just hold you, or do you want help and advice?' – **Jackie Wells**

'Never ever EVER have a child go to bed, or leave for school with bad vibes between you. The bedtime one can be resolved with a little time, but I ALWAYS exercise extreme patience when they get ready for school. There's nothing more yucky than having to face a school day feeling sad.' – **Candice Slabbert**

'You are always a safe space when they're in trouble. They should never feel that their only option is catastrophic or dangerous. That yes, they will be in trouble if they do something stupid, but less trouble than if they didn't feel they could call you.' – **Candice Firmani**

'Anchors for teens: No matter the twists and turns that life may bring, you can always count on Mom and Dad to be there for you. Don't compound any situation by lying to cover it up. Just tell us the truth. We can all figure it out together. For parents: Try to understand your child's perspective, even if you disagree … Empathy is everything.' – **Throshini Naidoo**

'When they're grown and have flown the nest, try to trust the good foundation which you know you built. They will come back to it. Also, don't waste time feeling sad that they don't call or communicate often enough for you – if you want to talk to them, you call them, even if it's always you taking the initiative. You've given them wings and they're flying – don't try to pull them back to you. They will come of their own accord.' – **Nikki Ramsbottom**

'You're only as happy as your unhappiest child.' – **Theresa Gibbon**

'Remember you are their safe soft place to land. Know when to stop pushing them, we all have to pause and reset in life.' – **Gail Dublin**

'1. Sometimes "No" is a full sentence. 2. As your teens become adults it's lovely to have those moments with them when they get adult humour and dish out sarcasm, and tell outrageous jokes – but sometimes they're still little people who need a hug and a cry. Enjoy both.' – **Beth Williamson Moody**

When they're pushing boundaries

Parenting teens is different from parenting toddlers, but one thing holds true for both: boundaries make them feel safe. Adjust your rules for older kids and trust the foundation you've put in place during their younger years. It's a great idea to get their input about the values in your home, the non-negotiables and the consequences for overstepping. Then, when they play up, stay calm and apply the agreed consequences.

'1. Boundaries and consequences must be put in place. 2. Learn to say YES to reasonable, age-appropriate requests (particularly from teens), let go of your fears and let them have fun growing up. If they abuse that privilege and/or trust, refer to (1) above!' – **Leanne Clarke Ross**

'Teach your kids to think in terms of real life consequences for their actions from a very young age. This means taking Mom or Dad's anger and disappointment off the table as a consequence for something that they do (or don't do) and making them think about what could happen that closes doors to their future instead. A thought-up punishment is not a real life consequence … Losing the WiFi is only a real life consequence if they abuse something to do with WiFi. If you … then … is the consequence. Parenting like this makes our children unafraid to discuss their "failures" with you

because they understand that "failures" are only markers to show us where we need to adapt our behaviour. Real life consequences teach them to think before acting. It's a wonderful life skill. Finally, respect begets respect, kindness begets kindness – bullying begets a bully, screaming begets screaming etc … Our children and their behaviours are the real life consequences of our parenting inputs.'
– **Hedwig Claire Scheepers**

'Stop nagging. As the late New Zealand social justice advocate Celia Lashlie said in the start of her iconic talk, "Parenting Boys:" Shut up, shut up, shut up and shut up … you all nag too much.'
– **Katrien Dehaeck**

'Parenting is relentless but worth it. Consistent yes and no, so that your children know where they stand. Boundaries need to be firm but flexible … they allow a child to feel secure but they need to adjust as children grow. It takes a village to raise a child – find your tribe and share the load. Adulting is hard. Being a kid is hard. Make time for hugs and grace.' – **Gabi Milne**

'When your teen boy is rude, take a breath. See your child as that three year old they once were. Feel that immense love and acknowledge that that beautiful child who adored you is still inside. Then bring some genuine curiosity to the situation and say, "I hear you … I'm really interested to know what you think about what just happened and what that says about the adult you are becoming. Does it make you proud? Don't answer me now. Think about it. And when we're both calm come back and tell me." This is from Megan de Beyer's book *Raising Men* – paraphrased and misquoted. I only ever had to say that once and it flipped our relationship around. I guess it reminds them that we aren't just Mom, or the nearest, easiest, safest punching bag, but humans they love and still adore. It holds up a mirror they need to look into, and helps them choose a different path forward.'
– **Ann Ellis Brown**, admin

Unconditional love

The world is a tough place for our kids. The knowledge that no matter what anyone else thinks of them, no matter how they mess up in their age-appropriate risky behaviour, you still love them and have their back, is another of the greatest gifts we can give a kid.

'Unconditional love amidst the daily struggles, lows and highs. Respect your children. Apologise when you have messed up, made a mistake or when you are just plain wrong about something. Where there is love, anything can be fixed, sorted, solved.' – **Khalida Speck**

'Spend time teaching your children empathy. please. It's a gift to the world.

'Don't say NO to everything, but what you do say NO to, stick to!

'Life doesn't owe you anything but you owe it to yourself to do your best.

'Read to and with your child, a lot!

'Give lots of hugs. Say I love you, a lot! And always say sorry when you need to, and mean it, they will see how meaningful and important these words are.

'They need to lose sometimes, it's not always their turn to shine. Know how to celebrate others too.' – **Shaney Merifield**

'All that stressing, and pushing and nagging about my child's marks at school was mostly about me. I wanted to boast that my child was a straight A student. As soon as I let that go and became satisfied if he was putting in an effort with his studies and passing, our relationship changed. And after all, no one has ever asked me what I got for maths, history, science etc. when I was in Grade 7, 10 or 12! Let them enjoy their childhoods without all this pressure!' – **Giuliana Bland**

'The advice I would give is to accept them for who they are, guide but don't dictate and love them unconditionally.' – **Jo Facey Pentz**

'Love them , even when you don't like them. Pick your battles. Let them make decisions from young – eg. What do you want to wear today? Before we go, do you want to play on the swing or the slide?

How do you want your haircut? It gives the kids some degree of control of their life and as they get bigger the decisions get bigger too.'
– **Amanda Letecia**

Your best is good enough

Stop trying to be perfect – it's not possible. Some days you'll win at parenting and some days you'll suck. Aim for good enough.

'The one that really stuck with me was, 'As soon as you say "My child would never", here they come nevering like they never nevered before.' We are imperfect humans raising imperfect humans and mistakes are part of the journey. It's how we navigate them together, and learn from them that counts.' – **Angela Hannah Linnetts**

'1. Have a sense of humour. 2. Don't take anything they say or do personally. 3. Coffee and red wine are essential to make it through the teen years. 4. Have a good group of friends to lean on and remind you that this too shall pass. 5. You did good, they do good, and they will do so because you love them and showed up.' – **Lisa Van Deventer**

'This was the best advice I got when I was trying to be the perfect mum to my firstborn 20 years ago. I think it saved my parental sanity. Let your children grow up seeing you make mistakes, be vulnerable or have an argument. Within limits, of course. And also let them see how you fix the things you are not proud of. If children never see their parents doing anything "wrong" they will grow up thinking that they have to be perfect and that is one helluva pressure. It is human to fluff up and tools for dealing with that are as important a skill to give your kids as accepting that they can and will fluff up. Show them it is ok to be human. Be a real parent, not a perfect one. Otherwise your children will think they have to be perfect. Don't put that pressure on them or on yourself. My advice? The most basic: "Just love them forever. 🤍🤍🤍" That's all anyone needs. Someone who loves them forever.' – **Kate Couzens Bohlin**

'Everyone will always make the best decision for themselves (and their children, family etc.) in the moment. It might not be the best decision in hindsight or a decision that others would also make but that doesn't actually matter. Do what you feel is best at the time and know that that is good enough.' – **Malika Hepburn**

'For all the new moms: Advice you receive is generally coming from a good place but honestly take and use what you want, ignore the rest and do what's best for you and that might include ignoring all the advice you have been given. Do what works for you and your child.' – **Lisa Cass Stockwell**

'A long time ago, I was struggling with my health and had 2 little kids under 18 months. I was given a great piece of advice – just remember that all the stages are short lived. So if anything in child rearing is worrying you it will be over shortly. I used this advice until they were 20. Always have dinner together, with no phones. And if anyone in the family is struggling, ask each family member to share their highs and lows of the day. Gratitude is huge!' – **Debbie Harris**

'If you have messed up, say sorry. Keep it simple. Not only are you validating them, you are also modelling.' – **Sheila Valentini**

'1. Just remember that no one else knows what they're doing either. (We often spend our time judging ourselves against either an impossible standard or against other parents who seem to have it all figured out. In truth, everyone is just figuring it out as they go along.) 2. Don't let other people make judgements about your child (or you) when they haven't walked a mile in your shoes. People see your life from their perspective, which leads to them making assumptions. 3. Everything shines in its own time. There is no timetable for life. Timetables are for classrooms, not for people.' – **Lesley Scott**, admin

'These words, which I think were taken from Steve Jobs talking at Stanford University, are the ones I try to live by: "Live each day as if it was your last. Your time is limited so don't waste it living someone else's life. Have the courage to follow your heart and intuition – they somehow already know what you truly want to become, everything else is secondary". I also read the *Desiderata* often. I especially like the part that goes: "You are a child of the universe, no less than the trees and stars; you have a right to be here. And whether or not it is clear to you, no doubt the universe is unfolding as it should". While raising my daughter I reminded myself often of what CG Jung wrote which is: "Nothing has a stronger influence psychologically on their environment and especially on their children than the unlived life of the parent". I do love what Elizabeth Gilbert wrote in her book *Eat Pray Love*: "Little girls who make their mothers live grow up to be such powerful women". I didn't really care about my life until my daughter came along. When my daughter was born I started to make a real effort to sort myself out so that I didn't pass my dysfunction onto her and so these words really resonate with me.' – **Morganna Pearse**

'Always try your best, even if your best is not as good as somebody else's.' – **Janice Roberts**

'Children learn by watching what their parents do. Be a good example.'– **Cheryl Hunkin Patrick**

'1. Tell them the truth. They see it anyway. They see you. Be present. 2. Give rational reasons for rules and restrictions. Not just " because I say". 3. Teach them manners, kindness and respect by example. 4. Don't judge, don't shame – listen, empathise, support – but teach them that all actions have consequences. 5. Forgive yourself. Move on and do the next right thing. – I succeed in implementation of the above about a third of the time but hey I am a mother and perhaps – especially in our crazy, edited, airbrushed, social media world – the most important thing they need to know is that no-one is perfect – or we all are in our imperfection.' – **Miriam Bosky Wheeldon**

Divorce

It's so, so hard – hard on you, hard on your ex, hardest on your kid/s. After years of discussions on The Village around this topic, the best advice is summed up by Caryn below:

'Single/divorced moms and dads – keep the relationship with the other parent friendly in front of the child/ren at all times. Never bad mouth the other parent in front of or to the child – the child sees

themselves as 50% mom and 50% dad so when one parent is always degraded or "trashed" the child inherits the thought that the 50% related to that parent is also bad … Best advice I ever got when I ended up as a single mom, not easy especially in early days of a relationship breakup but it's ALWAYS about the best interest of the child.'
– Caryn Meyer

Listen to listen

Similar to being present in the moment but worth its own section of advice is the art of really listening, and giving what you hear the weight of deep thought and a considered response. Strong connections are what keep our kids safe – they will weigh up their behaviour based on their connection to you. Make time to listen to them, really hear who they are becoming and what their hopes and dreams are for the future.

'Mine is no matter what s#%t is going down, listen and listen some more. No advice, no providing solutions, just open, non-judgmental listening. Sometimes very hard to do but it's created amazing trust and intimacy with my kids.' – **Zann Hoad**

'Have good thoughts of your children, show them you care by listening to them. Tell them how amazing they are, and that you know they will prosper in life. Really make them feel important by asking them for advice on challenges you face – this will make them feel empowered. Include them in discussions that affect their lives, hear what they have to suggest. Encourage and motivate them. They will live to be all that we speak into their lives.' – **Soraya Sanders Abrahams**

'My very recently learnt lessons from fighting with a child: In a fight we often listen to have a response, and we don't listen to hear what the other person is saying. At the same time, a fight is often a trigger for people to say things that they normally keep to themselves, because they know it is not "appropriate" or "the right thing to say". But if a theme comes up again and again, it's a thing. Sit down to understand where it comes from (either from the parent or the child's side) and figure it out.' – **Phillippa Barnard**

'For a long time I would hear my son but not REALLY listen. When I started to REALLY listen we were able to engage better together and oftentimes I was able to consider a different perspective – his perspective. It built a much deeper trust between us and has stood us in good stead during the teenage years.' – **Caroline Peirce**

1. 'When you feel you are in the middle of a terrible storm/crisis with your child or they are in a particular phase just remember "This too shall pass".
2. Love, love and love some more, even if they appall you. If they feel your disappointment in times of their crisis it just spirals further. And everyone needs love and hugs. It just makes the world go round so much smoother!
3. Try to listen rather than fix (my worst fault).
4. Teach them manners and respect from a very early age. The upbringing my kids had in SA reinforced by school has created incredibly polite and much loved kids. Americans always comment on how they are so respectful.
5. How they present to you is not necessarily how they present to the outside world. We are a safe space to behave really badly!
6. Trust is a process. They need to earn it. One step at a time (especially night curfews)!
7. In a particularly dark time in one of my teen girl's life she came to my room, as I lay on the bed sobbing thinking what a failure as a parent I was, and she said "You know none of this is your fault".' – **Justine Lang**

'Be curious. About who they are; what makes them tick; how they feel; what they think; why they behave in certain ways; what they choose; how they make decisions; the world they live in; how they plan to solve problems and achieve their goals. This means creating space to listen and ask questions; allowing them to make mistakes and learn from them; belief in their abilities and encouragement, rather than removing all obstacles and fixing. Plus: Insist on respect – for themselves, other people, and their physical and natural environments. This means modelling appropriate behaviour!' – **Frances Campbell**

'Don't push your dreams onto your children. Let them realise their own dreams. Listen carefully because sometimes they are so keen to please you that they get into a wrong career that can ruin their lives.' – **Careena Bernstein**

Get the focus right

Breathe. Pause. Pick your battles.

'I received a great piece of advice right here on The Village. In the eye of the storm, protect your relationship with your teen. That has helped me overreact less, pick my battles better and remember that this too shall pass.' – **Romy De Jager**

'Don't sweat the small stuff and this too shall pass …' – **Stefanie Minnaar**

'A piece of advice I often give is pick your battles. And what I learned through raising three teens was to walk away and not engage in a slanging match (I screamed into my pillow instead) – to practise the pause.' – **Jane Dawson**

'Choose your "No" carefully. Do not fall into the habit of just saying no, they will assume you'll say no and not ask, rather find a way to do it without your knowledge. Pick the thing you'd be willing to go to war for as your hard no. Let everything else be a negotiation.' – **Lyndsay Nash-Beresford**

'Find ways to say "Yes".' – **Penny Foyn**

'Focus on what you can control and let go of the things you can't.' – **Shahiema Rylands**

'Pick your battles has been my motto since the day my son was born. Nobody is perfect, you can't get everything right. Decide what is really important and focus on that. E.g. I decided I would never nag my child about clothes. Let him wear what he wants, even if it doesn't fit or match. And if you don't want to wear shoes, also fine.' – **Anneke Bosman**

'I once received advice about following the 10-10-10 approach. It's a simple philosophy that goes like this: When you are making any decision or dealing with a tricky situation, whether in your personal, family or business life consider how the course of action you want to take will make you feel ten minutes from now, ten months from now and, finally, ten years from now. And will it even matter?' – **Karen van der Berg**

'Don't waste the little time you have with them fighting over homework. That's their responsibility. If they don't do it, it is no reflection on your mothering.' – **Riva Lange**

'When my friends ask me why I am so chilled with my teen and tween I say I live by *The Serenity Prayer*: "God grant me the serenity to accept the things I cannot change; courage to change the things I can; and wisdom to know the difference." But it is that last line that is soooooo important.' – **Liesl Lotter**

'Everything happens for a reason, and always at the right time it's meant to happen (used when impatience rears its head).' – **Judy Huddlestone Snyders**

'Remember who is the adult and who is the child. Even if you don't feel like an adult, try and act like one. Sometimes that means taking a beat to remind yourself, walking away instead of engaging in a screaming match no matter how hot your blood is boiling. Be like a duck: frantically paddling below but always calm on the surface. Oh. But also. Don't be too duckish. Let them see you cry, and fight, and struggle, and get through stuff. They do need to know that you are human too.' – **Kim Penstone**, admin

'When you or your kids become overwhelmed, add water. Take a sip of water, take a bath, go for a swim, splash some water on your face …' – **Chantelle Correia Vd Bijl**

'Whatever decision you make, ask the question: "Am I minding my own business?" – in other words, is this my place/battle/truth/etc?

If not, move on. Take care of all things relevant to you.' – **Annemie Neethling Zuidema**

'Prioritise your partner, then the children. If you don't nurture the original relationship, the rest will suffer. Love and education are the biggest gifts you can give your children.' – **Philanie Jooste**

'With the youngest turning 16 soon and the eldest almost 23, my most sage advice is: just breathe! Everything will be fine in the end.' – **Suzanne Smith Du Plessis**

Useful resources

There is a saying from the United States, 'If mama ain't happy, ain't nobody happy'. Definitely the same for when papa ain't happy. Parenting can be one long exercise in having old wounds ripped open and coming face to face with our worst selves. Not everyone can or wants to go to therapy, but some inner work is required. These are some places to start.

The University of California, Berkley offers a free 11-week course in applying positive psychology to your life. The course is called 'Science of Happiness'

https://www.edx.org/learn/happiness/university-of-california-berkeley-the-science-of-happiness

Read Dr Kristin Neff's book *Self-compassion: The Proven Power of Being Kind to Yourself*. She also offers free guided self-compassion meditations on her website at www.self-compassion.org

We live in a country that is deeply traumatised and we all carry the trauma in our bodies to some degree or another. Understanding what physical trauma is and the effects it has on behaviour is a step towards healing. Trauma researcher Bessel van der Kolk wrote a book called *The Body Keeps The Score* (2014), drawing on his 30 years of research and clinical experience in treating trauma.

Dr Gabor Maté speaks and writes simply about healing, addiction, trauma and relationships between parents and children. As a starting point, his website is helpful: https://drgabormate.com

Villagers often refer to the work of Brené Brown, who became famous after her TED talk on the power of vulnerability. Start there, and then follow her wherever you do your social media. Oprah Winfrey and Bruce D Perry's *What Happened to You? Conversations on Trauma, Resilience and Healing* is another useful resource in this area.

Another Village favourite is Mel Robbins, whose podcast is aimed at creating a better life. She uses the most recent research to talk about how to do that. The podcast can be found where you usually listen to podcasts or you can follow a link from her website: https://www.melrobbins.com

If teenagers seem impossible to understand, it's because their brains are stretching and forming. To understand how physical this is, download this excellent PDF from a British school that breaks it down and offers simple advice for frustrated parents. The document also provides a further reading list: https://www.bohuntsixth.org/wp-content/uploads/2021/02/The-Teenage-brain.pdf

Villagers advise following Whitney Fleming on Facebook for her articles and motivations to help confused, tired and frustrated parents of teens: https://www.facebook.com/whitneyflemingwrites

There are excellent online resources for parents who want to understand current thinking about gender issues and learn the language they can use to talk to their teenagers. A starting point is reading an article on gender-responsive parenting, which can be found here: https://www.unicef.org

The Genderbread Person we used in this book comes from a website called 'It's Pronounced Metrosexual'. It's an endless resource for parents and teachers, containing many free downloads and edugraphics.

For a deeper understanding of the history of queerness, a wonderful book for teenagers and parents alike is *Queer: A Graphic History* by

Meg-John Barker (2016), with illustrations by Julia Scheele. It makes a great gift for a querying teenager.

When it comes to parenting teens, many, many answers to questions posed on The Village come down to 'listen'. We think we know what it means to listen, but often we do not. A very short explanation is given by Simon Sinek in a five-minute explanation here: https://www.youtube.com/watch?v=qpnNsSyDw-g

An oldie but goodie is a book called *How to Talk So Kids Will Listen & Listen So Kids Will Talk* by Adele Faber and Elaine Mazlish (2013).

An excellent way to connect with children is always through play. For teens and their parents, a great game to play together is called We're Not Really Strangers. The game is about 'empowering meaningful connections'. There are various packs of the game. Any of them can be used, but be warned that the one that is for friends contains some questions about sex, so you may want to remove those when playing with your family to avoid desperate cringey moments between questioner and answerer.

Tech can be the bane of our lives but we have two outstanding resources in South Africa for negotiating boundaries and understanding legalities. The first is the resource-packed website Klikd, which is owned and run by The Villagers who helped out with information in our tech chapter. Just about any question you have regarding tech seems to be answered at https://klikd.co.za

Emma Sadleir and Tamsyn de Beer wrote a book called *Don't Film Yourself Having Sex*, which might be a little outdated now, but if it passes through your hands, don't miss the opportunity to read their simply laid-out advice for staying safe.

The blog on Emma Sadleir's website has all kinds of useful articles around law and tech. It's an excellent resource: https://www.thedigitallawco.com

She's also written a great book called *Selfies, Sexts and Smartphones: A Teenager's Online Survival Guide* (2017).

If educating yourself about money feels daunting, you really must read Sam Beckbessinger's book *Manage your Money like a F*cking Grownup: The Best Money Advice You Never Got* (2018). And once you've read it, find the version she wrote for teens, called *Manage your Money Like a Grownup: The Best Advice for Teens* (2020). No one does it better. Her tone and explanations come from a place of not having understood how money worked herself.

If you don't yet have your will sorted, there is a week each year in which some lawyers offer the service for free. You can find out when (it's different every year) and more from the Law Society of South Africa, whose website is https://www.lssa.org.za

If you want to trick yourself into saving money, consider getting the Stash app. It 'sneaks' money into a savings account based on parameters you give it. You can do R10 a day. You can let it save money for you based on how much you exercise. And there's even a button for saving when there's loadshedding. The amounts that go off are so small, it's possible to not miss them. But then one day you have a domestic emergency and you open your Stash account to find you have R4 359 in it, which is like manna from heaven. Many Villagers have eased the Christmas-season money leaks with their Stashes.

A budgeting tool Villagers like is the 22seven app.

A very up-to-date and thorough book that is useful to any parent with a child at school, any educator and any learner is *Basic Education Rights Handbook: Education Rights in South Africa* (2022), which is the result of very careful and thorough work by the people at SECTION27, who work in the area of social justice. The book covers school fees, pregnancy, disability, religion, sexual violence, corporal punishment and so much more that affects guardians and children at school in South Africa. The chapters are also available online here: https://section27.org.za/resources/section-27-publications/basic-education-handbook/

Useful resources

And finally, here's a list of crisis resources for adults and teenagers in South Africa:
- Find a Helpline, a directory of crisis hotlines: https://findahelpline.com/countries/za
- South African Depression and Anxiety Group (SADAG): WhatsApp 31393 or call 0800 567 567
- Akeso Crisis Helpline: 0861 435 787
- Gender Violence Helpline: 0800 150 150
- loveLife youth hotline: 0800 212 900
- Triangle Project (LGBTQI+): 021 712 6699
- Tears Foundation: *134*7355# or 010 590 5920
- LifeLine: 0861 322 322
- Substance Abuse Helpline: WhatsApp 32312 or call 0800 12 13 14
- Childline: 116
- Alcoholics Anonymous: 0861 435 722
- Rape Crisis: 021 447 9762

Acknowledgements

From Vanessa

Fifty-six thousand grateful thank yous, to my 60 000 best friends, our wonderful Village parents and co-authors! The members of The Village role model all the values our children need to thrive, daily: kindness, tolerance, a willingness to listen and learn. Patience, positivity and strength. Wisdom, humility and resilience. Of course, there would be no book without them. If I said thank you 60 000 times it wouldn't be enough.

So much love and gratitude to The Village Admin and Creative Team, past and present: Megan de Beyer, Ann Ellis Brown, Kim Penstone, Kirsty Peters, Lesley Scott, Neesa Moodley, Danielle Hervey, Christine Le Roux, Zama Pienaar, Mari Sciarappa-Lerche, Vicki Sleet, Karin Joubert, Dale Rudolph, Heidi Sulcas, Clint Hendricks, Nicolas James, Jasmine Tasriet, Kayla Tess Pattenden.

To our two magnificent, supportive and steadfast Boost Crews. Two-hundred-plus people is too many wonderfuls to mention by name – but for all you do, all day, every day, thank you from the bottom of my heart.

To Karin Schimke: What an inspiration you are as an adventuring, wise and lovely co-author. Thank you!

Thank you to patient, professional and clever Gill Moodie – our dream publisher, who believed and held steady. You are the most superb Book Parent. I hope our baby makes you proud!

And to my own precious family: Sim, Jenny, Natasha and especially my Gremlins, Milla, Max and Leo. I know being the offspring of 'That Lady from The Village' was mortifying – but I promise you, you wouldn't be so wonderful without it.

... and from Karin

Having been a work-from-home person since my children were born and not just since COVID, I'm a little embarrassed to say that there were days when my daytime social life was the sum total of The Village. I'd have to remind myself I couldn't talk about things that happened in The Village at supper time. The Villagers seemed so real and so close to my life, and so many of you so vivid in mind, that you felt like my colleagues. And now look, you became my colleagues in the real sense in this book! So first and foremost, I'd like to thank and acknowledge my general co-workers for always keeping me challenged, entertained and actively engaged with the job of parenting.

Then, I'd like to acknowledge Vanessa for having such a clear sense of what The Village represents and for always screwing her courage to the sticking place when it comes to keeping things as balanced and fair as is possible. I don't know how you do it, but it's awe-inspiring to watch. I know it's not easy either and that it takes its toll. Thank you for all the bullets you dodge and all the ones you take to keep this Village shining brightly.

About the authors

KARIN SCHIMKE works as an author, editor and writing coach and, in her journalism years, was a parenting columnist for *Femina* magazine and Parent24. She has won commendations for her journalism, and awards for her work as a poet and translator. She is the author of the weekly *Love Letter* tracking her adventures in her post-parenting years now that her children are out of the house. She writes about books and reading on her Instagram @readingdarling.

VANESSA RAPHAELY started her career on London's Fleet Street, moving on to the world of women's magazines before returning to South Africa to become the multi-award winning editor of *Cosmopolitan* and to run Associated Media (publishers of *Cosmopolitan*, *House and Leisure*, *Marie Claire*, *O, The Oprah Magazine* and

IMAGE BY LEIGH PAGE

others.) After 20 years, she left and launched The Village, South Africa's most beloved and influential social media platform for families of tweens, teens and young adults. She has written children's books and a novel (*Plus One*, published in 2019.) She writes widely, both locally and internationally, on travel and is a reluctant public speaker. Vanessa lives in Cape Town with her husband, her youngest, Leo, and her two dogs. Her daughter, Milla, works happily in the art world and her eldest boy, Max, is completing his software engineering degree in Scotland.